Ludovic Kennedy was bo[...]
and educated at Eton and Christ Church, Oxford.
At the age of twenty he joined the Royal Navy
Volunteer Reserve and in his seven years of service
rose from the rank of Midshipman to Lieutenant,
and as a Sub-Lieutenant in a destroyer narrowly
missed an encounter with *Tirpitz* off Norway.

Mr Kennedy is well known for his appearances
on television as presenter or introducer on such
current-affairs programmes as *The World at One*,
24 Hours, *Midweek* and *Tonight*. He has also
made a number of films for television including
Scapa Flow, *Battleship 'Bismarck'*, *The Life and
Death of the 'Scharnhorst'*, *The U-Boat War*,
The Rise of the Red Navy and the acclaimed
Target 'Tirpitz'. He is the author of several books,
including *Nelson's Captains*, *Sub-Lieutenant:
A Personal Record of the War at Sea* and the
highly-praised bestseller *Pursuit: The Chase and
Sinking of the 'Bismarck'*.

MENACE
The Life and Death of the *Tirpitz*
LUDOVIC KENNEDY

SPHERE BOOKS LIMITED
30–32 Gray's Inn Road, London WC1X 8JL

First published in Great Britain by
Sidgwick and Jackson Limited 1979
Copyright © Ludovic Kennedy and Sidgwick and Jackson
Limited 1979
Published by Sphere Books Ltd 1981

For Stephen Roskill
with admiration and affection

Printed and bound in Great Britain by
©ollins, Glasgow

CONTENTS

Preface

There have been several books on the battleship *Tirpitz*, but this is the first that has been able to draw on the rich store of naval 'Ultra' signals, that is, signals to and from German naval units and bases during the war that were decrypted by the famous codebreakers of Bletchley Park. Strictly speaking the term 'Ultra' was a top security classification, attached to paraphrases of the decrypts that were sent to carefully selected officers for their information, and ensuring that they would not be seen by anyone else. But since the story was released a few years ago, the word 'Ultra' has come to be used in a generic sense for all intelligence obtained by our cryptanalysts, and it is in this sense that I have used it in this book. (I have been told that the reason the story was kept secret for so long is that for many years after the war several countries continued to use the German Enigma machine, which coded 'Ultra' signals, and for a long time we were able to decrypt for our own use their diplomatic and military telegrams. Enigma, I understand, is now obsolete.)

The full story of how Ultra helped us win the war at sea still remains to be written, although Patrick Beesly, in his fascinating book *Very Special Intelligence*, has already made a notable contribution. In researching for this small book it has been a revelation to me to what extent Ultra helped us in the naval war in Norway, where *Tirpitz* was stationed for almost her entire career. Indeed, one wonders where we would have been without it. It was Ultra that provided us with the intelligence that enabled our forces to torpedo the heavy cruiser *Prinz Eugen* in February 1942; to divert the convoy PQ 12 out of *Tirpitz*'s way in March 1942; to launch a torpedo attack against *Tirpitz* the following day; to sink the *Scharnhorst* in

December 1943; and to launch the successful Fleet Air Arm attack on *Tirpitz* in April 1944 at a time when she was at her most vulnerable. From Ultra we also learned of the success of the X-craft attack on *Tirpitz* in September 1943, of the Fleet Air Arm attack on her in April 1944, and of the Lancaster attacks in November 1944, all within hours of their happening. Paradoxically it was the faulty appreciation of Ultra in July 1942 (the intelligence that *Tirpitz* was on her way to Altenfjord during the passage of Convoy PQ 17) that led to one of the greatest British naval disasters of the war.

There can be little doubt that we could have achieved even more with Ultra had there not sometimes been a considerable time-lag between the transmissions of the German signals and their arrival, decrypted, at the Admiralty's Operational Intelligence Centre in London. In the light of everything we did achieve, it is astonishing that German intelligence never rumbled to the fact that we had broken their codes. When I talked to Admiral Dönitz near Hamburg a few years ago, he assured me that, despite several enquiries, they were convinced we had not done so.

I have used as illustrations transcripts of several Ultra signals that were of benefit to us in the naval war in Norway. I would have liked also to include photostats of signals from the many brave Norwegian agents such as Björn Rörholt, Magne Hassel, Torstein Raaby and Egil Lindberg who kept watch on *Tirpitz* at her various anchorages and contributed so much to the success of our operations against her, but I have been informed that these signals are either unobtainable or unavailable.

I am most grateful to the following who have helped me in preparing material for the book and/or in reading the manuscript: Patrick Beesly, David Brown, Rear-Admiral Godfrey Place, Professor Dr Jürgen Rohwer, Björn Rörholt, Captain S. W. Roskill, and David Woodward; to the BBC for permission to use quotes and stills from my television documentary programme 'Target Tirpitz'; to my secretary, Joyce Turnbull, for much correspondence; to her niece, Hazel Plenderleith, for the speed and accuracy of her typing; and to Mrs Mary Pain for her valuable help with research.

'It was accurate intelligence which made all else possible.'
Captain S. W. Roskill, *The War at Sea*

1. Fleet-in-Being

On the evening of 4 May 1941 Captain Karl Topp, commanding officer of the new German battleship *Tirpitz*, then alongside in the harbour of Gdynia, Poland, sat in his cabin thinking what to say next day to his Führer, Adolf Hitler. Through the open door that led to the big dining and conference room he could see the Führer's photograph and, next to it, a portrait of the white-bearded Admiral von Tirpitz, creator of the German Navy. From his cabin porthole Topp could see *Tirpitz*'s sister-ship *Bismarck* lying gracefully at anchor in the bay and, near her, the new heavy cruiser *Prinz Eugen*, named after Marlborough's ally in the war of the Spanish succession.

Topp had taken command of *Tirpitz* at Wilhelmshaven on 25 January 1941 – almost two years after Tirpitz's grand-daughter Frau von Hassel, in the presence of Hitler and his court, had launched her from the stocks (a debt which Hitler was to repay in 1944 by executing her husband, then ambassador in Rome, for his part in the 20 July plot). With his firm, square features and thick bull-neck Topp looked like what he was, a tough professional sailor; Charlie, his men called him, with affection and respect. He had spent his early career in U-boats and destroyers, and had the reputation of driving *Tirpitz* like a destroyer. His crew recalled with pride how he had manoeuvred *Tirpitz* into the harbour at Gdynia with the assistance of only one tug, while Lindemann in *Bismarck* had called for fourteen.

Tirpitz and *Bismarck* were then the largest, fastest battleships yet built; *Tirpitz* at 52,600 tons fully laden was even bigger than *Bismarck*, at 50,900 tons. Both ships were massive, yet elegant, with their humped superstructures, wide beams, and raked funnels and bows. Both were over

11

a sixth of a mile long, could steam at 31 knots, mounted eight 15-inch guns in four twin turrets, carried four to six aircraft and a crew of ninety officers and 2300 men, and had a network of watertight compartments. No German had seen these ships without pride, no neutral or enemy without admiration.

But, as Topp knew, there was one important difference between them. *Bismarck* had already completed her long sea and battle trials, and was now under orders for Atlantic operations – that was why the Führer was coming tomorrow. Many of *Tirpitz*'s trials were still to come. Soon *Bismarck* and *Prinz Eugen*, under Admiral Günther Lütjens, would sail for a three-month cruise on the Atlantic trade routes. There, supplied by oilers and supply ships in secret rendezvous, they would endeavour to cut the precious lifeline from America that enabled Britain, and Britain alone, to continue the fight against Germany. It would be a repetition on a grander scale of Lütjens' foray earlier that year with the battlecruisers *Scharnhorst* and *Gneisenau*, which during a two-month cruise had sunk 116,000 tons of Allied shipping.

After that cruise Lütjens had taken the two battle-cruisers into Brest, and it was Raeder's intentions that in May they should join *Bismarck* and *Prinz Eugen* in mid-Atlantic, there to act as a powerful combined force. If the plan had succeeded, who knows what havoc they might have caused. But luck was not with the Germans. First the *Scharnhorst* was found to need lengthy dockyard repairs, then in April *Gneisenau* was seriously damaged in a brilliant RAF torpedo-plane attack; repairs to her would take six months. *Bismarck* and *Prinz Eugen*, thought Topp, were still a formidable force; but if *Tirpitz* were to join them, they would surely be invincible.

That evening the Führer's special train left Berlin, arrived at Gdynia in the morning. He and his entourage embarked in the yacht *Hela* and steamed out to where *Bismarck* was lying in the roads. Admiral Lütjens received him on the quarter-deck with the naval, not the Nazi, salute. After inspecting the ship and discussing with Lütjens the coming operation, Hitler returned ashore. In the afternoon Lütjens received him again on board *Tirpitz*, introduced him to Topp. Entertaining Hitler in his cabin, Topp chose his moment carefully. 'I beg you, my Führer, to allow *Tirpitz* to accompany *Bismarck* and *Prinz Eugen* on the coming Atlantic operation.'

Perhaps Topp had hoped that Hitler, having seen the power of *Tirpitz* for himself and desirous of a great naval victory, might readily grant the request. Perhaps he knew the answer would be negative, but felt he had nothing to lose by trying. Hitler nodded but said nothing. He knew little enough of naval affairs and seemed to care less; matters of this kind were best left to Raeder. And Raeder, Topp knew, would never allow any ship to become operational before completing the long and rigorous training programme the German Navy always demanded.

Thirteen days later, from the bridge of *Tirpitz*, Topp watched with envy as *Bismarck* and *Prinz Eugen* weighed anchor and sailed to the westward; Operation RHEINÜBUNG ('Rhine Exercise') had begun. For a few days there was silence; then, in succession, news of triumph and disaster. First, Admiral Lütjens' victory in the Denmark Strait, the sinking of the famous British battlecruiser *Hood* and the damaging of the brand-new battleship *Prince of Wales*; later, the crippling of *Bismarck* by a lucky torpedo hit only 400 miles from Brest and her destruction next day by superior British forces under Admiral Tovey. And Topp wondered, as he was entitled to, whether, despite *Tirpitz*'s lack of battle training, her presence might not have resulted in the sinking of *Prince of Wales* as well as *Hood*, and in Operation RHEINÜBUNG having a glorious instead of a tragic ending.

And so, through the summer and autumn of 1941, in the enclosed waters of the Baltic and away from the attention of British bombers, *Tirpitz* continued her sea and battle training. There were main armament practice shoots at the target ship *Hessen* (a pre-Dreadnought battleship), anti-aircraft shoots at drogues towed by aircraft, torpedo firings (unlike *Bismarck*, *Tirpitz* had torpedo tubes mounted amidships), damage-control exercises, the launching and recovery of the Arado seaplanes. And in order to acclimatise the crew to battle conditions in the Atlantic, for several weeks she remained permanently at sea, topping up with fuel and supplies from oilers and merchantmen.

For Topp and his crew it was hard work. But there was often the lighter side. One day at anchor they were passed by the U-boat U-556, commanded by Lieutenant-Commander Herbert Wohlfarth. Wohlfarth as junior officer, saluted; Topp, from the deck of *Tirpitz*, returned the salute. Then Wohlfarth shouted up, 'Captain, do as I do!' Topp waited; and the U-boat promptly dived.

Only once did *Tirpitz* have to stand by for operational activities. In June Hitler attacked Russia, and in September, as a result of German intelligence, a large task force consisting of *Tirpitz*, the pocket battleship *Admiral Scheer*, light cruisers, minesweepers and destroyers stood by near the Aaland Islands for a sortie by the Russian fleet. In the event the Russians stayed put in Kronstadt, where they were to remain for most of the war.

Meanwhile, what role was *Tirpitz* to play once her training was complete? Despite what had happened to *Bismarck*, Raeder and the German naval staff were still keen for her to attack trade on the high seas. There was a plan (originally proposed by *Tirpitz*'s navigating officer, Commander Bidlingmaier) for her and the heavy cruiser *Hipper* to proceed by way of the English Channel (thus avoiding the northern passages and the British Home Fleet at Scapa Flow) to Brest, there to join *Scharnhorst, Gneisenau* and *Prinz Eugen* for commerce raiding in the Atlantic. Such a force would have been even more powerful than that proposed for the *Bismarck* operation in the spring.

But Hitler vetoed it. The loss of *Bismarck* had greatly shaken him, and a repetition of that disaster would be intolerable; in addition, the warships in Brest had already suffered severely from air attacks which would inevitably be stepped up if *Tirpitz* joined them. In this Hitler was supported by Lütjens' successor as fleet commander, Vice-Admiral Ciliax, and by the flag officers of Naval Groups North and West.

So instead Raeder proposed that *Tirpitz* should sail to Norway, where she would be well placed to attack the convoys carrying British war supplies to northern Russia. This was much more to Hitler's liking. Ever since the British commando raids on the Lofoten Islands and Vaagsö in the spring and summer of 1941 he had been obsessed with the idea that sooner or later Britain was going to invade Norway, so the more her seaward defences could be strengthened the better. 'Every ship that is not in Norway,' he said in December 1941, 'is in the wrong place.'

A *Tirpitz* task force in Norway would serve other purposes: safeguard the important supplies of iron ore and nickel coming down from north Norway; discourage British naval attacks on German-controlled coastal shipping; and most important of all, act as a fleet-in-being, a menace, that would tie up British battleships at Scapa Flow. Even so, Hitler had qualifications. *Tirpitz* was only to sail to Norway if the naval staff could guarantee that she would arrive undamaged (the pocket battleship *Lützow* had been damaged by aircraft torpedo en route to Norway in June), and she was not to attack convoys to Russia when it was known they were supported by carriers.

Early in 1942 the naval staff gave the necessary undertakings, and orders were issued for *Tirpitz* to sail for Trondheim, where a snug berth had been prepared for her at the end of Foettenfjord, forty miles from the sea. When

Bismarck had sailed for Norway from the Baltic, she had been routed through the Kattegat and Skagerrak, but Raeder, suspecting that her passage had become known to enemy agents (he was right, both Swedish naval intelligence and a Norwegian resistance group had reported her to London), ordered her to sail via the Kiel Canal. She passed through the canal on 12 January. Two days later, in thick weather and with an escort of destroyers, she sailed from Wilhelmshaven, and on 16 January reached, without incident, her berth at Foettenfjord, under the lee of a big hill.

An Ultra intercept next day apprised the British of her arrival (though planes failed to find her until a week later). For them it was grim news. *Tirpitz* was now poised on the edge of the Atlantic battlefield, and if she came out, the stroke of luck that had led to the cornering of *Bismarck* could not be expected again. In fire-power and defensive armour the modern British battleships were fully a match for her. But with a top speed of nearly 30 knots she was faster than any of them; and unless she could be slowed up by torpedo attack, she would always have the advantage of being able to pounce on convoys at will and retiring immediately out of danger in the face of battleship opposition.

Earlier the British First Sea Lord had written of the necessity of having always three modern battleships available (two at sea, one refitting) to cope with her. Now Winston Churchill, the Prime Minister, wrote, 'The destruction or even crippling of this ship is the greatest event at sea at the present time. No other target is comparable to it. I regard the matter as of the highest urgency and importance.'

2. A Missed Opportunity

After nearly a year of exercises and training, morale in the *Tirpitz* is high. The crew had faith in their captain and ship and now, at their operational base at last, they longed for the opportunity to test themselves and her in action. But, as Topp told them, there would be no chance of a sortie for the time being. The German Navy was desperately short of destroyers (half the entire force had been sunk at Narvik in 1940), and the five that had escorted *Tirpitz* to Trondheim and without which she would be unprotected against enemy submarines were needed for duties elsewhere. What not even Topp knew was the nature of those duties: to proceed to Brest, there to pick up *Scharnhorst*, *Gneisenau* and *Prinz Eugen* and, in accordance with Hitler's directive, to escort them back to Germany via the English Channel.

So, at her bleak anchorage among the whitened hills, protected to seaward by a curtain of anti-torpedo nets and by anti-aircraft batteries on the slopes above, *Tirpitz* settled down to a life of temporary inactivity. Yet in a large warship there is always much to be done: decks to be scrubbed, messes to be cleaned, stores to be embarked and stowed, guns to be exercised, engines to be lubricated, instruments of all kinds to be trained and tested. And in attending to the wants of the 2400 men who had made their home in her, a small corps of cooks, butchers, storekeepers, doctors, dentists, laundrymen, physical training instructors, welfare officers and others all found their time occupied.

Shore leave was granted to a third of the crew at a time. At first there was little enough by way of diversion: walks along the lonely road that skirted the edge of the fjord.

shopping for sealskin slippers and Norwegian sweaters in the village of Foetten, bartering drink or tobacco rations for fresh milk and eggs at neighbouring farms. Later a ski school was started on a nearby slope, and this proved very popular. The Swedish frontier was only sixty miles away, and officers in civilian clothes were allowed to cross over in small groups for meals of steak or salmon, or to buy luxuries like silk stockings and scent, then almost unobtainable in Germany.

It was in the long, dark evenings that time hung most heavily. But Topp and his executive officer, the pro-Nazi Commander Düwel (he had a photograph of Hitler in his cabin), were tireless in organizing entertainments. There were concerts by the ship's band, nightly film shows, lectures by the officers, boxing matches and, occasionally, concert parties sent from Germany. The medical officer, Dr Kiel, presented a puppet show with costumes, characters, decor and stage made by himself. Many of the men played the accordion or mouth organ and there were regular sing-songs in the messes. There was a well stocked library, supplemented by books from an old Elbe steamer which carried comforts to garrisons between Stavanger and the Arctic Circle. And a few sailors, in the hope of improving their standard diet of beans, potatoes and meat, braved the cold and dark to lower baited lines to passing cod.

By the beginning of February 1942 *Tirpitz*'s destroyers had reached Brest, and on the night of the 12th, in company with *Scharnhorst*, *Gneisenau* and *Prinz Eugen*, they put to sea under the new admiral commanding battleships, Vice-Admiral 'Black Otto' Ciliax. Hitler had refused to let them return to Germany via the Atlantic because of what had happened to *Bismarck*. The passage through the Channel would be within spitting distance of the English coast, but there were no British battleships nearer than Scapa Flow, and there would be Luftwaffe air cover all the way.

The operation was a brilliant success. British intelligence had realised what was afoot, but it was thought unlikely that the German squadron would leave Brest at night and so make the passage of the Straits of Dover by day. Because of this and other mishaps the ships were not spotted until crossing the Bay of Seine next morning. Belated attacks by torpedo-planes, torpedo-boats and destroyers were all beaten off, and it wasn't until they were abreast of the Dutch coast that *Scharnhorst* and *Gneisenau* were damaged by mines, though not enough to prevent them reaching harbour. 'Nothing more mortifying to British sea power,' thundered the London *Times*, 'has happened since the seventeenth century. Vice-Admiral Ciliax has succeeded where the Duke of Medina Sidonia failed.' A few weeks later *Gneisenau* was heavily damaged by bombs while in dry-dock, and took no further part in the war; but *Scharnhorst* would become operational again after repairs.

Meanwhile, the German Admiralty lost no time in furthering Hitler's directive that warships not in Norway were in the wrong place. A week after reaching Germany, Admiral Ciliax hoisted his flag in the *Prinz Eugen*, and, in company with the pocket battleship *Admiral Scheer* (which in 1940 had carried out raiding operations in the Atlantic and Indian Oceans) and the destroyers *Hermann Schoemann, Friedrich Ihn* and Z-25, sailed for Trondheim. They reached Grimstad Fjord south of Bergen next morning, the same anchorage to which *Prinz Eugen* had escorted *Bismarck* on the eve of the ill-fated Rheinübung nine months before, and weighed for Trondheim in the evening. Ultra intercepts of their sailing orders from Naval Group North reached the Admiralty in time for four submarines to take up position at the entrance to Trondheimsfjord. There, early next morning, the *Trident* hit the *Prinz Eugen* with one torpedo, severely damaging her stern and rudders; but, with the assistance of the destroyers, she managed to limp into Trondheim.

One of a number of decrypted signals from Naval Group North (Gruppe Nord) to German warships concerning the imminent departure of the *Prinz Eugen* and *Admiral Scheer* from Bergen to Trondheim to join *Tirpitz*. It reached the British Admiralty in time for the submarine *Trident* to take up position at the approaches to Trondheimsfjord, and there hit the *Prinz Eugen* with a torpedo early the next morning.

22 February 1942

TOO   1602/1619

FROM: GRUPPE NORD
TO: U 377

REF. W/T MESSAGE 1214: PROCEED VIA SQUARE AF 53 TO SQUARE AF 5870, AND ACT THERE AS FLANK ESCORT FOR PRINZ EUGEN, ADMIRAL SCHEER, 5 DESTROYERS WHICH ARE TRANSFERRING TONIGHT OR VERY SOON FROM BERGEN TO TRONDHJEM. ASSUME THAT ENEMY AIR AND NAVAL FORCES WILL OPERATE. REPORT SIGHTINGS. YOU ARE FREE TO ATTACK TARGETS DEFINITELY RECOGNISED AS ENEMY. W/T WATCH SERVICE 'A'.

The signal from Vice-Admiral Ciliax, flying his flag in *Prinz Eugen*, reporting on the damage done by *Trident*'s torpedo. This signal arrived decrypted in the Admiralty Operational Intelligence Centre the following afternoon.

23 February

TOO   0933

FROM: ADMIRAL COMMANDING BATTLESHIPS

MOST IMMEDIATE

PRINZ EUGEN TORPEDOED BY S/M OR AIRCRAFT. RUDDER OUT OF ACTION. 10 METRES BLOWN AWAY ASTERN. ENGINE INSTALLATION STILL EFFECTIVE. AM PROCEEDING IN TO TRONDHJEM.

German naval grid chart carried by all warships and used for reference positions at sea (see Ultra signal opposite).

With escorts now available to protect her, *Tirpitz* was once more ready for operations, and early in March one came to hand. A long-range Focke-Wulf reconnaissance plane sighted the Russia-bound convoy PQ 12 near Jan Mayen Island, and the German Admiralty approved the proposal of General-Admiral Rolf Carls, Flag Officer Naval Group North, at Kiel, to attack it. On the evening of 6 March *Tirpitz*, with Ciliax's flag at the fore, and preceded by the three destroyers, passed down Trondheimsfjord and into the open sea. There she was sighted by the patrolling submarine *Seawolf*, who at once radioed to London; by midnight her report was in the hands of the British Commander-in-Chief, Home Fleet, Admiral Sir John Tovey, who, with the battleships *King George V* and *Duke of York*, the battlecruiser *Renown*, the carrier *Victorious* and a destroyer screen, were just 100 miles from PQ 12 and ready for any eventuality.

This was the moment Admiral Tovey had been waiting for, ever since hearing that *Tirpitz* had completed her training in the Baltic and moved to Norway. Nor did it come as a surprise, for the news of the return of *Tirpitz*'s destroyers to Trondheim combined with an Ultra intercept of the Focke-Wulf's sighting of PQ 12 made an enemy sortie seem very probable. For him and the men of the Home Fleet, who for so long had endured the discomforts of long patrols in winter weather and the austerity of life at Scapa Flow, this was a moment full of promise. Nine months earlier Tovey had watched his flagship *King George V* and the battleship *Rodney* pound *Tirpitz*'s sister-ship *Bismarck* to destruction. Now he was being given the opportunity to bring off the spring double, to remove at a stroke the menace that threatened British seaborne trade, and to release for service in the Indian Ocean battleships to take the place of the sunken *Prince of Wales* and *Repulse*. Would the God whom he believed in so fervently favour him again? He waited anxiously for further news.

Tirpitz and her destroyers, steaming at 23 knots, headed north-east along the Norwegian coast until about midnight, then turned due north. The seas were rough and the weather bitterly cold. By 10 a.m. next day Ciliax reckoned he was in a position to fly off two Arado sea-planes to search for the convoy, but snow showers and severe icing made this impossible. Instead he decided to detach his three destroyers to search to the north-north-west while the flagship searched to the north-west.

Tovey, meanwhile, had been steaming north-eastwards through the night in order to place his force between *Tirpitz* and the convoy. At about the time that Ciliax was detaching his destroyers, Tovey was intending to fly off a search by some of *Victorious*'s aircraft. Had this taken place, *Tirpitz* would have been spotted that morning, and attacked by torpedo-planes soon after. But, as with the Arado seaplanes, icing prevented it.

This was the first occasion during this complex operation when, but for a mischance, the two sides would have made contact. The second occurred that afternoon. At noon PQ 12 and the homeward-bound QP 8 passed through each other's lines in a snowstorm. Two hours later the German destroyer Z-25 passed only ten miles to the westward of QP 8 but failed to locate it. In the middle of the afternoon Z-25 sighted smoke to the north, which turned out to be a Russian straggler from QP 8, the *Izhora*. *Friedrich Ihn* hit her with one torpedo, and as she sank was rejoined by *Tirpitz*. At this time Admiral Ciliax's force was some seventy-five miles north-west of PQ 12 and 150 miles north-east of Tovey and the Home Fleet.

The *Izhora* had managed to send off a distress signal before going down, which Tovey's radio operators had picked up. A signal made on enemy transmission a little later and fixed by direction finding led Tovey to think that the German force had now abandoned its mission and was returning to base. He therefore detached his destroyers to search along a line between the *Izhora*'s last position and Trondheim, but in case he was wrong took the fleet north-eastwards towards Bear Island to act as a covering force for the convoy. He maintained this course until midnight, then turned south to be within supporting distance of his destroyers, and to fly off a search by *Victorious*'s aircraft in the morning.

Ciliax, meanwhile, had failed to find the convoy where he expected it (the Focke-Wulf reconnaissance plane had underestimated its speed by some 2 knots). But, far from turning south for home, as Tovey imagined, he now decided to begin a fresh search for the convoy ahead of its expected line of advance. He turned his force to the east, in which direction the convoy was moving, and went on to 25 knots.

Ciliax's destroyers were by now very short of fuel. In the evening he detached the *Friedrich Ihn* to Narvik with orders to oil and rejoin his flag. During the night the force reduced to slow speed, and two attempts were made to refuel *Hermann Schoemann* and Z-25 from *Tirpitz*'s bunkers. But heavy seas and icing made this impossible, and after the hoses had parted twice the two destroyers were ordered to oil at Tromsö.

At 7 a.m. next morning (the 8th) Ciliax ordered Topp to turn north, in the direction of Bear Island, until three hours later he had reached a position estimated to be ahead of the convoy's likely path of advance. Here *Tirpitz* reduced speed, turned to the south-west and, with the ship's company at action stations, zigzagged in the direction in which it was thought the convoy was steering. What he was not to know was that as a result of Ultra intercepts PQ 12 had been re-routed much farther north, and he missed it by some eighty miles. But for this an encounter would have been almost inevitable, and with only a light force escorting the convoy, and Tovey's battlefleet 200 miles away, *Tirpitz* could have wreaked havoc.

For Tovey was by now moving away from Ciliax, and on much the same course. Having concluded that *Tirpitz* was returning home, he was taking the Home Fleet towards Iceland to collect fresh destroyers, his own being very short of fuel. It wasn't until the early evening of the 8th that he received a signal from the Admiralty, based on Ultra intercepts, that *Tirpitz* might be in the vicinity of Bear Island. Accordingly at 5.30 p.m. he reversed the course of the fleet and headed north-east.

Tirpitz searched unsuccessfully all day along PQ 12's expected route, and at about the time Tovey was turning towards him Ciliax decided to abandon the operation and take *Tirpitz* home. German signals indicating this were also decrypted, and their contents passed to Tovey in the early hours of 9 March. On receiving them he immediately altered course from north-east to south-east. Had he received this intelligence earlier, he might have been within gunshot range of *Tirpitz* by the morning.

However, all was not yet lost. At 6.40 a.m., when *Tirpitz*, now rejoined by *Friedrich Ihn*, was some 115 miles east-south-east of Tovey, and some 100 miles west of the Lofoten Islands, the carrier *Victorious* flew off six aircraft to search a sector to the south-east; and a squadron of twelve torpedo-carrying Albacores, with engines warmed up, were ranged on the flight deck ready for take-off.

At eight o'clock that morning *Tirpitz* was steaming south at 25 knots, with the white mountain tops of the Lofoten Islands abeam to port. In his charthouse just off the bridge the navigating officer, Commander Bidling-maier, was writing up his log; Topp was resting in the nearby look-out room, Ciliax had just gone off for break-fast in his quarters aft. Having laid off the course for Trondheim, Bidlingmaier calculated they would be back in their berth by early evening.

It had been, he reflected, a disappointing operation: they had burned a vast quantity of oil fuel, with nothing to show for it but one small Russian steamer. Nor had matters been helped by a series of indecisive signals from Berlin and Naval Group North about the ship putting in to either Tromsö or Narvik. He himself had proposed to Topp the night before that Tromsö would be a better permanent base than Trondheim, as it was nearer the Russian convoy route.

His thoughts were interrupted by a cry of 'Aircraft astern'. He dashed on to the bridge and, as senior officer present, told Lieutenant Kühnen, the officer of the watch, 'Go on to 30 knots. Prepare ship's aircraft for launching.' The alarm bells were sounded, and throughout the ship men not already closed up ran to their action stations. Topp appeared, approved what had been done, then Ciliax. They knew that the enemy plane must be carrier-based, no land-based plane having the range, and that a torpedo attack must be imminent. Perhaps the Arado could drive off the shadower before the striking force arrived. Ciliax said: 'As soon as we've launched her, we'll run east for the shelter of Vestfjord and Narvik.'

Sub-Lieutenant T. T. Miller, piloting the Albacore that had spotted *Tirpitz*, sent off a sighting report, which was received with joy in the fleet, especially by the aircrews of *Victorious*'s Albacores, now only waiting for take-off. 'God be with you,' signalled Tovey to the captain of *Victorious*, 'a wonderful chance.' The twelve planes took off one by one and disappeared to the south-east.

Leading the striking force was Lieutenant-Commander W. J. Lucas, who took his planes up to 3500 feet in order to approach *Tirpitz* through cloud and, as he hoped, unseen. At 8.30 the Arado took off, and immediately after, Miller, now joined by two other shadowers, saw *Tirpitz* turn east. But the Arado's foray was unsuccessful. It attacked all three shadowers in turn, wounding one observer in the leg, then, its ammunition expended, flew off in the direction of Bödö.

For Lucas and his pilots, now only twenty miles astern of *Tirpitz*, the chances of a successful attack seemed good. The Albacores, which had recently joined the fleet, were faster and better planes than the old Swordfish which had brought *Bismarck* to book the year before; cloud conditions were favourable, and there was only one escorting destroyer. Against this was the fact that Lucas had only recently joined the squadron and had never flown with his fellow pilots before. Further, the squadron had been given no recent opportunity to carry out vital practice runs on ships of the Home Fleet.

At this time the laid-down method for attack by twelve torpedo-planes was to reach a position well ahead of their target, there to split into four sub-flights of three; simultaneously, half of these sub-flights would attack the enemy's port and half the starboard bow. They would thus cover a 90-degree arc, so that whichever way the enemy turned there would be a good chance of some torpedoes hitting.

But Lucas abandoned this plan while still approaching his target. Because *Tirpitz* was steaming at 30 knots into a 35-knot wind, the 100-knot Albacores were overtaking her at no more than a mile every two minutes. Worried about icing conditions and being out of visible contact with his sub-flights, Lucas signalled them to attack independently. This gave freedom of manoeuvre, but lost them all the advantages of a co-ordinated approach.

At 9.17 the squadron broke out of cloud to find Lucas's sub-flight of three planes about a mile on *Tirpitz*'s port beam, with the other three sub-flights to starboard of her. As she hadn't opened fire Lucas thought, wrongly, that he hadn't been observed, and that an immediate attack now might pay better dividends than one from ahead when her gunners would be fully prepared. So he gave the order to dive; his three planes levelled out close to the water and released their torpedoes. But the range was nearly a mile, double that recommended.

Signal from Admiral Sir John Tovey, C.-in-C. Home Fleet, sent in the early hours of 9 March 1942 to the aircraft carrier *Victorious*. Admiral Tovey had just received from the Admiralty the Ultra intercept from Naval Group North giving the position of *Tirpitz*'s rendezvous with her destroyers (see pp. 34–36) off the Lofotens.

SECRET

NAVAL MESSAGE

From: C-in-C HOME FLEET
To: VICTORIOUS
(R) GENERAL

Cypher
Method
Light

AIDAC

Expect TIRPITZ in position 068° 15′N. 010° 38′E. at 0700A/9 steering to Southwards. Report proposals.
0316/9 March 1942

Reply from *Victorious* to Admiral Tovey setting out proposals for torpedo bomber attack.

SECRET

NAVAL MESSAGE

From: VICTORIOUS
To: C-in-C HOME FLEET

Cypher
Method
Light

AIDAC

Propose fly off searching force of six aircraft at 0630 to depth of 150 miles sector 105 to 155 degrees. Fly off striking force of 12 as soon as ranged about 0730. Ship maintain present course and speed after searching force flies off till 1000 then turn to 315 degrees 26 knots. Fighters remain with ship. Consider 12 aircraft maximum that can be ranged in present weather.
0537/9 March 1942

Tovey's last signal to *Victorious* before the unsuccessful attack.

NAVAL MESSAGE

From: C-in-C HOME FLEET
To: VICTORIOUS

A wonderful chance which may achieve most valuable results.
God be with you.
0721/9

Tirpitz, meanwhile (and *Friedrich Ihn* too), had opened up a tremendous barrage with heavy guns, smaller guns and close-range fire. Topp calmly watched the torpedoes drop, then amid the din shouted to the helmsman, 'Hard a port!' But Ciliax, who had commanded the *Scharnhorst* before the war, had other ideas. 'No!' he shouted, 'hard a starboard!' The helmsman waited, but not for long. 'I am in command of this ship, sir, not you,' bellowed Topp, 'Helmsman, obey my orders. Hard a port.' The wheel went over, the ship heeled to starboard as she swung to port. With relief *Tirpitz*'s bridge party saw the torpedoes miss a long way astern.

The leaders of one of the other three sub-flights, seeing Lucas's attack and anticipating *Tirpitz*'s turn to port, crossed to her port side to be in a better position to attack himself. Three minutes after Lucas's attack his own sub-flight released their torpedoes. Once again they all missed astern.

Tirpitz's turn to port, however, had improved the positions of the two remaining sub-flights, enabling them to move ahead of the ship by cutting the corner. At 9.25 these six planes came in together on the battleship's starboard bow, covering a 45-degree arc. But by now *Tirpitz*'s gunners had found the range, and as she swung to starboard two planes were shot down in the act of releasing their torpedoes. One of them, carried forward by its own momentum, hit the sea just ahead of the ship, and from the wing of the bridge Bidlingmaier saw the pilot climb on to the tail-piece and give a wave, as the battleship thundered by.

Of the remaining four torpedoes fired, three missed comfortably, but the fourth passed only ten yards from *Tirpitz*'s stern. Had this one been aimed just a fraction of a degree further forward, then the *Bismarck* story — when a torpedo from a Swordfish had jammed her rudders and brought her almost to a standstill — might have become

Tirpitz's story as well.

By 9.27 it was all over and the Albacores, except for the two casualties, were on their way back to the fleet. In *Tirpitz* the decks were littered with empty shell cases: in ten minutes of action the ship had fired more than 4500 rounds of ammunition, in addition to two broadsides from the 15-inch guns (Lieutenant Kühnen, standing too near the blast from one of these, was partially deafened for life).

Reports from all stations reached the bridge: no torpedo hits or damage; three men wounded from the Albacores' machine-gun fire. Relief and gratitude enabled Ciliax to make amends to Topp for his earlier extraordinary behaviour. 'Well done, captain,' he said, 'you fought your ship magnificently!', and as a commander-in-chief in the field, empowered to make immediate awards, he took off his own Iron Cross and pinned it on to Topp.

Two hours later the ship was running up Vestfjord, there to be joined by Z-25 and *Hermann Schoemann*, and by fighters from Bödö whose presence would have been welcome long before. At five in the evening she anchored in Bogen Bay, close to Narvik. She stayed there three days, during which Allied submarines took up waiting positions between Vestfjord and the approaches to Trondheim.

At last orders came for Topp to sail for Trondheim in the early hours of Friday 13 March, but being a superstitious man he gave orders to weigh at 11 p.m. on 12 March.

In pitch darkness and with an escort of five destroyers *Tirpitz* steamed down Vestfjord at 30 knots, then turned south along the coast. At 1.30 a.m. a flotilla of British destroyers from Scapa Flow, acting on intelligence from Ultra intercepts, closed the coast between Bödö and Trondheim, and turned north.* They and *Tirpitz* were now approaching each other at a mean speed of 60 knots.

* One of these destroyers, which had just returned to Scapa with *Victorious*, was HMS *Tartar*, in which the author was serving as a sub-lieutenant.

But at 3.30 a.m. the British ships had to turn for home, so as to be clear of the coast and enemy aircraft by dawn. *Tirpitz* entered their search area six hours later and, having avoided all the waiting submarines, entered Trondheimsfjord. Next day she was back in her berth in Foettenfjord.

ULTRA INTERCEPTS RELATING TO *TIRPITZ*'S SORTIE AGAINST CONVOY PQ 12

A selection of just a few of the decrypted Ultra signals, mostly from Naval Group North (General-Admiral Rolf Carls at Kiel) to Admiral Commanding Battleships (Vice-Admiral Otto Ciliax, flying his flag in *Tirpitz*) concerning the operations of *Tirpitz* and the destroyers *Friedrich Ihn*, *Hermann Schoemann* and *Z-25* against the Arctic convoy PQ 12. Intelligence from this source enabled the British, firstly to re-route PQ 12 out of danger, secondly to attack *Tirpitz* with torpedo-planes as she was returning to Trondheim.

It should be remembered, however, that because of varying time-lags between the interception and decryption of the Ultra signals, only some reached the Admiralty in time to be of immediate operational use.

5 March 1942

1. TOO   2208

   FROM: ADMIRAL COMMANDING NORTHERN WATERS

   MOST IMMEDIATE

   AIR RECONNAISSANCE 1300/5. CONVOY 15 LARGE STEAM SHIPS, SMALL ESCORT, COURSE 030 DEGREES 6 KNOTS SQUARE AA 9918.

---

6 March

2. TOO   0048

   FROM: ADMIRAL COMMANDING BATTLESHIPS
   TO: 5TH DESTROYER FLOTILLA AND T.5 FOR 2ND TORPEDO-BOAT FLOTILLA.

   BE AT 3 HOURS READINESS FROM 0900/6.

---

3. TOO   1637

   FROM: GRUPPE NORD

   TO: ALL VESSELS

   IMMEDIATE

   ADMIRAL COMMANDING BATTLESHIPS WITH TIRPITZ AND THREE DESTROYERS WILL LEAVE SQUARE AF 6717 AT 1700/6/3 NORTHBOUND AT 25 KNOTS TO OPERATE AGAINST CONVOY.

4. TOO   2107

   FROM: GRUPPE NORD

   TO: ADMIRAL COMMANDING BATTLESHIPS

   AIR RECCO EARLY ON 7/3 HAS BEEN ARRANGED
   NORTH OF 62 DEGREES NORTH AND WEST OF 17
   DEGREES EAST, CONCENTRATING ON SQUARES AB
   82, 83, 91, 85, 86, 94 AND ON CONVOY.

German rendezvous positions ('Square AF 6717', etc.) refer to
the grid charts (see page 21) covering German naval operational
areas, and with which all sea-going vessels of the German Navy
were issued. Only the first two figures relate, the last two refer
to detailed positions within the square which are not shown on
the chart reproduced on page 21. The British Navy captured
one of these grid charts early in the war.

---

6 March

5. TOO   1759

   FROM: GRUPPE NORD

   TO: U-BOATS 454, 403, 377

   TAKE UP POSITIONS IN RESPECTIVE SQUARES AC 43
   UPPER HALF, AC 43 LOWER HALF, AC 46 UPPER HALF
   WITH UNRESTRICTED PERMISSION TO ATTACK. DO
   NOT CROSS TO THE WEST OF 26 DEGREES EAST.

(*Tirpitz* would be operating West of 26 degrees East.)

6. TOO   1446

   FROM: ADMIRAL COMMANDING U-BOATS
   (PERSONAL)

   TO: ADMIRAL COMMANDING NORTHERN
   WATERS (PERSONAL)

   JUDGING FROM THE EVIDENCE I HAVE RECEIVED I AM
   OF THE OPINION THAT THE CONVOY WILL ALREADY
   HAVE PASSED THE POSITION TO WHICH THE U-BOATS
   HAVE BEEN ORDERED. I SHOULD SHIFT THE
   DISPOSITION FURTHER EASTWARDS TO CATCH THE
   CONVOY BY DAY ESTIMATING THE CONVOY'S SPEED
   OF ADVANCE AT 7 TO 8 KNOTS.

(The Admiral Commanding U-boats was Karl Dönitz.)

7. TOO 2042

   FROM: GRUPPE NORD

   TO: ADMIRAL COMMANDING BATTLESHIPS

   IMMEDIATE

   CONVOY ROUTE IS BELIEVED TO RUN
   APPROXIMATELY FROM SQUARE AB 7150 TO AC 4196
   TO 5176 TO 5553 TO 6748 OR FARTHER NORTH AS FAR
   AS ICE LIMIT. IF IT APPEARS OPERATION WILL TAKE
   YOU EAST OF 26 DEGREES EAST, SEND SHORT
   SIGNAL IN GOOD TIME ON AMOUNT OF U-BOATS.

---

8 March

8. TOO 1153

   FROM: GRUPPE NORD

   TO: ADMIRAL COMMANDING BATTLESHIPS

   (1) ESTIMATE CONVOYS SPEED AT 6 TO 8 KNOTS,
   TODAY IN SEA AREAS SQUARES AB 5970, 5510, 6210,
   6590, TOMORROW AT 0800 IN AB 6590, 6210 AC 1760,
   4560.
   (2) I ESTIMATE THAT THE LENGTH OF TIME DEVOTED
   TO THE SEARCH SHOULD NOT EXTEND BEYOND
   NIGHTFALL ON 9/3. THEN RETURN TO TRONDHEIM.

(Signal 8, and others, showing the Luftwaffe's and *Tirpitz*'s plan of search, helped the convoy to be routed clear of danger.)

---

8 March

9. TOO 1927

   FROM: GRUPPE NORD

   TO: ADMIRAL COMMANDING BATTLESHIPS

   (1) DESTROYER FLOTILLA HAS REPORTED INTENTIONS
   OF ACB.
   (2) WE SUGGEST YOUR CONTINUING TO SEARCH BY
   DAY ON 9/3.
   (3) REPORT BY 2300 TODAY NEW R/V OF TIRPITZ WITH
   TWO TROMSO DESTROYERS BY SHORT SIGNAL.
   GROUP NORTH WILL THEN PASS ON NECESSARY
   ORDERS TO DESTROYERS.

10. TOO   2150

FROM: GRUPPE NORD

TO: 5TH DESTROYER FLOTILLA, SCHOEMANN,
Z-25

ABC WILL CONTINUE OPERATION ON 9/3. JOIN
TIRPITZ AT 0800 IN SQUARE AC 4735.

---

11. TOO   2209

FROM: GRUPPE NORD

TO: FRIEDRICH IHN

REMAIN IN NARVIK FOR THE TIME BEING. 3 HOURS
NOTICE FOR STEAM.

---

12. TOO   2332

FROM: GRUPPE NORD

TO: ADMIRAL COMMANDING BATTLESHIPS

HEREBY ACKNOWLEDGE SHORT SIGNAL
CONCERNING BREAK-OFF OF OPERATION AND R/V IN
SQUARE AF 3185.

13. TOO   2327

    FROM: GRUPPE NORD

    TO: Z-25, SCHOEMANN

    CONTRARY TO W/T MESSAGE 2150, ACB IS
    BREAKING OFF OPERATION. RENDEZVOUS 0800/9
    SQUARE AF 3185.

(These last two signals, following on No. 9, and pinpointing
Tirpitz's rendezvous with her destroyers, reached Admiral Tovey
in the early hours of 9 March. They led him to alter course at
once towards the rendezvous and resulted in the sighting of
Tirpitz and subsequent attack on her by *Victorious*'s Albacores.)

8 March

14. TOO   2359

    FROM: GRUPPE NORD

    TO: FRIEDRICH IHN

    ADMIRAL COMMANDING BATTLESHIPS WILL
    PROCEED FROM R/V AT 0800 IN SQUARE 3185 TO R/V
    AT 1400 IN SQUARE 6183 THEN FROHAVET.

(*Friedrich Ihn* joined *Tirpitz* at the new 0800/9 rendezvous, but
Z-25 and *Schoemann*, left up at Tromsö, signalled they could
not reach it in time. As a result they were not with *Tirpitz* when
the Albacores attacked. Frohavet: the approaches to
Trondheim.)

9 March

15. TOO   1301

    FROM: ADMIRAL COMMANDING BATTLESHIPS

    TO: GRUPPE NORD

    AT 1020 MASS TORPEDO ATTACK BY 20 TO 25
    SWORDFISH. BY SKILLED AVOIDING ACTION IN
    SPITE OF ATTACKS BEING PRESSED HOME TO
    500–800 METRES, THE TORPEDOES WERE AVOIDED. 3
    AIRCRAFT SHOT DOWN.

(In fact the attacks were made by twelve Albacores, they were
not pressed home, and two not three of the aircraft were shot
down.)

16. TOO   1135

    FROM: GRUPPE NORD

    TO: 5TH DESTROYER FLOTILLA, Z-25,
    SCHOEMANN, TORPEDO-BOATS 5 AND 12.

    ADMIRAL COMMANDING BATTLESHIPS IS ENTERING
    VESTFJORD. JOIN HIM FORTHWITH.

---

17. TOO   2247

    FROM: GRUPPE NORD

    TO: ADMIRAL COMMANDING BATTLESHIPS

    (1) INTEND TO LEAVE TIRPITZ AT NARVIK UNTIL LAP
    TO TRONDHEIM IS AGAIN CLEAR OF ENEMY.
    (2) UNTIL THEN ANTI-SUBMARINE HUNT IN
    VESTFJORD AND OPERATIONS BY GERMAN AIR
    FORCE AGAINST NAVAL FORCES, ABOVE ALL
    CARRIERS.
    (3) REPORT WHAT ROUTE THROUGH INNER LEADS
    YOU CONSIDER POSSIBLE FOR TIRPITZ.

---

12 March

18. TOO   2050

    FROM: GRUPPE NORD

    TO: ADMIRAL COMMANDING BATTLESHIPS

    (1) SAIL IF THERE IS NO LOCAL OBSTACLE.
    (2) RECOMMEND YOU BE AT THE NORTHERN
    ENTRANCE TO LANDEGO WITH YOUR FIGHTER
    ESCORT BY DAWN.

(*Tirpitz* arrived safely in Trondheim on the night of 13 March.)

3. British Precautions

On both sides, British and German, the PQ 12 operation had left its mark. The German Navy had set high hopes on it and, but for the Ultra intercepts that had given Tovey warning of *Tirpitz*'s likely area of search and enabled the convoy to be routed away from danger, the operation would almost certainly have succeeded. As things had turned out, the German squadron had used more than 8000 tons of scarce fuel, with nothing but the *Izhora* to show for it. Furthermore, the sudden appearance of the Albacores and their subsequent attack had come as a great shock to the Germans, and it was only Topp's skilful handling of the ship that had averted a major disaster.

In a report to Hitler, Admiral Raeder asked for two things: the completion of the aircraft carrier *Graf Zeppelin*, then lying abandoned in the yards at Gdynia, and the transfer to northern Norway of reconnaissance planes and bombers to seek out and attack British warships covering the convoys to Russia. Hitler agreed to both. The *Graf Zeppelin* order was later cancelled, when it was found she could not be operational in under two years, but a group of long-range reconnaissance planes and two squadrons of torpedo-bombers were ordered to airfields in northern Norway.

But Hitler made a further stipulation. Because of British carrier-based air power, *Tirpitz* could no longer be risked on prolonged operations at sea; her value lay in continuing as a fleet-in-being, a menace. From now on, he told Raeder, he would not give approval for *Tirpitz* to attack Russian convoys unless British carriers covering them had been located and neutralised. By this directive Hitler was committing *Tirpitz* – named after the founder of a deep-water navy – to a life of immobility in the Norwegian fjords.

Could the British Admiralty have known of Hitler's directive, they would have been spared much worry. It was true that Ultra had both saved the convoy and brought the Home Fleet to within a whisker of damaging, perhaps even destroying, *Tirpitz*, but such good fortune could not be relied on again. Despite Ultra, they had rarely known for certain where *Tirpitz* was or would be; they could only tell (because of the time-lag between interception and decryption) where she had recently been. In thick weather there was nothing to prevent her breaking out into the Atlantic unseen; and so worried was the First Sea Lord, Admiral of the Fleet Sir Dudley Pound, about the vulnerability of the Arctic convoys, that he submitted a memo to Churchill urging their temporary cancellation in the day-long summer months. But Roosevelt persuaded Churchill not to agree to this, and offered a US task force of a battleship and two cruisers in support.

Yet there were some measures which, in the early months of 1942, the British could and did take. A first essential, recognised as soon as *Tirpitz* arrived in Norway, was to have up-to-date information of her whereabouts, so that if she put to sea forces could be organised to attack her. The submarines stationed at the entrance to Trondheimsfjord and the reconnaissance planes that flew over the anchorage both reported regularly; but there would obviously be times when the submarines had to surface to charge batteries and the planes would fail to find *Tirpitz* because of the weather. Something more was needed,

It was to provide this that a brave young Norwegian by the name of Lieutenant Björn Rörholt was summoned from Stanmore, where he was helping some Poles make a miniature transmitter, to an appointment at the Admiralty. Rörholt, then twenty-one, with blue eyes and a mop of wavy hair, had lived in Oslo but had studied radio at the Trondheim Polytechnic. When the Germans invaded Norway, he was a cadet at the military academy. In the early days of the occupation he had put his knowledge to good use by sending radio messages to England, but in September 1941 a German detection unit surrounded his house in Oslo where he had been transmitting. He managed to shoot his way out and escape, first to Sweden, then to England. Because there was now a price on his head, the British agreed not to send him back to Norway during the war; he himself had said that he could not guarantee silence if interrogated under torture.

But exceptional times call for exceptional measures, and when it was explained to him that the Navy's most urgent requirement was for accurate and regular reports on *Tirpitz*'s whereabouts, he agreed to return to Trondheim and organise agents with transmitters. In late January, having dyed his hair black, he flew to Shetland and embarked in the fishing-boat *Arthur*, skippered by the famous Leif Larsen (who was to have his own involvement with *Tirpitz* later that year). With him went three transmitters.

Larsen dropped Rörholt at one of the outer islands, from where he took the regular passenger steamer to Trondheim. On disembarking a German soldier volunteered to carry his suitcase, containing the transmitters, and remarked how heavy it was! Rörholt obtained temporary lodgings with a friend, then went to see another old friend, Birger Grönn, manager of the dockyard, who had already obtained much useful information on the berth at Foettenfjord, which Rörholt transmitted to London.

Rörholt discussed with Grönn the best locations for the three transmitters, and it was agreed there should be one in the town itself, one at Foettenfjord, and one at Agdenes, at the mouth of Trondheimsfjord.

'We have a good man at Agdenes,' said Grönn, 'Magne Hassel. I know his brother Arne, and that he will help us. But there's a snag there. His house, which overlooks the fjord, is in a declared military zone.'

This didn't deter Rörholt. Having obtained temporary employment as an insurance salesman with the firm of Tobias Lund, he packed a cheap cardboard suitcase with policy documents, clothes, and, underneath, a transmitter. On arrival at Agdenes, he walked to the naval guardroom.

'My name is Rolf Christiansen,' he told the duty petty officer, 'I'm an insurance salesman. May I see the fort commander, please?'

He was taken to a friendly lieutenant-commander and explained his visit. 'I've come to see some clients who live here. I'm sorry I haven't got authority to visit from the Trondheim Kommandatur, but I've only just arrived from Oslo.'

'You sell insurance policies?' said the German. 'Then perhaps you can sell me one!'

Rörholt didn't know if he was joking. 'Unfortunately we are not allowed to take out policies on the lives of German officers. The risk is too great.'

The German laughed, then ordered a sailor to accompany Rörholt on his rounds. Hassel's was a small green house, and Rörholt noticed the splendid view of the fjord. He went inside, leaving the sailor at the gate. Hassel was expecting him, having already been briefed by his brother Arne.

'You will help?' asked Rörholt.

'Yes,' said Hassel, 'but I don't know morse.'

'You don't have to,' said Rörholt, pulling out a special card. 'Here is a very simple code. *This* is for *Tirpitz* putting to sea, *this* is for her returning, *these* are for the other ships. You understand?'

'Yes.'

'Good. Now let's find a hiding place for the transmitter before that sailor starts getting impatient.'

They found a place below the floorboards, in the foundations of the house.

'Goodbye, Magne,' said Rörholt, 'and good luck.'

Accompanied by the sailor, Rörholt returned to the base, where the friendly lieutenant-commander invited him to go by the fort's motor-boat to Trondheim.

Rörholt stayed on in Trondheim, recruiting half a dozen volunteers whose presence in the area would not be missed for five or six weeks, and who were sent by Shetland Bus to England for a short course in radio telegraphy. Then he went to Oslo to set up a similar network there. At the beginning of May he crossed over to Sweden, and was back in London a week later.

The next step for the British was to ensure that if *Tirpitz* did succeed in breaking out into the Atlantic, she would have no secure resting place on the French Atlantic coast. There was only one basin capable of holding her, the huge dock at St Nazaire, built for the great French passenger liner *Normandie*. A bold plan was initiated whereby an old destroyer, the *Campbeltown*, filled with three tons of amatol and escorted by eighteen motor gunboats and motor-launches, would sail five miles up the Loire estuary at night and ram the dock gates at speed. Delayed fuses to the explosives would later destroy both her and the dock. In the meantime Commandos would land to destroy the dock machinery.

The force left Falmouth on the afternoon of 26 March, and steamed south-westwards. Next day, in the Bay of Biscay, the escorting destroyers hoisted German naval ensigns. The weather was misty and overcast. At seven in the evening, when some seventy miles west-south-west of St Nazaire, the force altered course towards the Loire estuary.

At 10 p.m. a waiting British submarine signalled an accurate navigational fix, and just before midnight an attack on the port was made by a force of seventy Wellington bombers, so that the eyes of the defenders might be distracted upwards. Soon after, the force crossed the mudflats at the end of the estuary and, avoiding the swept channel, sailed into the Loire, with now no booms or minefields between them and their target.

Less than three miles from the dock search-lights were trained on them and a challenge flashed from the shore. A signalman in one of the motor-launches, chosen for his knowledge of German morse, flashed a Luftwaffe signal in reply, and while the Germans were digesting this *Campbeltown* signalled in German: 'Two ships damaged by hostile action request permission to enter harbour immediately.' This again gave the Germans pause for thought, and it wasn't until the force was less than eight minutes from the target that the Germans, at last realising they had been tricked, opened up with everything they had.

At such short range hits were registered at once, both on the light craft and on *Campbeltown*. But the Germans had left it too late, and going on to 18 knots for the last lap *Campbeltown* rammed the lock gates fair and square, then stuck fast in the breach she had made. The Commandos scrambled ashore, and there was fierce fighting as they tried to wreck the lock machinery.

With so many of the motor-launches and motor gunboats damaged or destroyed, it was impossible to rescue those who had gone ashore, and when the fighting was over what was left of the force started off downstream. Fourteen of the eighteen light craft were sunk or had to be scuttled, and of the 630 men who had sailed on the expedition 144 were killed and 259 taken prisoner. There were five awards of the VC.

Next morning, while a large party of German officers and men were inspecting the *Campbeltown*, the three tons of amatol in her forecastle went up with a roar. Other Germans panicked and, mistaking their own khaki-clad Todt labour force for British soldiers, began firing on them; French resistance forces, without orders, joined in. Altogether that morning some sixty German

43

officers and 320 men were killed.

For the British the raid on St Nazaire had been a great success – though, as Hitler had no intention of allowing *Tirpitz* to use the port, a somewhat empty one. Now the pressing need was to attack the ship herself. But how?

The quickest method was obviously air attack, and a fortnight after *Tirpitz* first arrived in Foettenfjord a strike by sixteen bombers was mounted against her; it aborted because of the weather. Not until two months later, on the night of 30–31 March, did a second attack take place by thirty-four Halifaxes. This was foiled by an extensive smokescreen, produced from canisters positioned round the fjord and released when it was known that enemy aircraft were approaching. Six bombers failed to return.

The next attack was on the night of 27–28 April when first twenty-six Halifaxes and ten Lancasters, then a second wave of eleven Lancasters, released bombs and mines, the latter designed to explode in the water at a depth of thirty feet. Again the smokescreen was highly effective in preventing the aircraft from seeing their target. Five were shot down.

One of these was piloted by Donald Bennett, later Air Vice Marshal Bennett of Pathfinder fame. 'I was hit fairly frequently before I reached the coast,' he said, 'and was a flamer before I got to *Tirpitz*. I saw her masts sticking out of the smoke as we went over, then the starboard wing folded up. I got out just in time. My chute opened just before I hit the snow.' Bennett and his wireless operator managed to avoid German patrols, and trudged through the night to Sweden.

Another crew member of a crashed plane was Ron Wilson, rear gunner of a Halifax. 'We went down to forty feet, the flak was coming both down at us, and up at us. I was firing at cliffs and boats as we went by. Then the skipper said, here's the *Tirpitz* now, and I went berserk on the guns, and sprayed the *Tirpitz* from stem to stern. The skipper shouted out, we've been hit, I'll try and get her over the mountain, which he did, and we landed on a frozen lake.'

The following night twenty-three Halifaxes and eleven Lancasters repeated the attack, which was again unsuccessful. Next morning Björn Rörholt, skirting the edge of Foettenfjord in the train to Sweden, noted that *Tirpitz*, and the heavy cruiser *Hipper*, which had arrived a week earlier both appeared undamaged. Four hours later he radioed this information from Fornöfoss, where he left the train to walk to Sweden.

This was the last aircraft attack on *Tirpitz* for some time. The German defences, particularly the smoke-screen, had proved too strong. Eleven valuable bombers had been lost with no damage to *Tirpitz* at all. Other methods of destroying her had to be found.

In fact two other methods, both by submersibles, had been in the experimental stage for some time. One was the 'human torpedo' or 'chariot', which the Italians had used with great success in their attack on the battleships *Queen Elizabeth* and *Valiant* in Alexandria harbour in December 1941. The chariot was the same size as a 21-inch torpedo with a 600 lb detachable warhead. Two men rode it, the one in front operating the rudders and hydroplanes, his companion navigating, negotiating the nets, and fixing the warhead to the enemy's hull. When submerged, with the two men wearing watertight clothing and a special breathing apparatus, the chariot's battery-driven motor had a speed of 3 knots and an endurance of 18 miles. A prototype chariot was built in April 1942, and a training programme was now under way in a Scottish sea loch, directed by Commander G. M. Sladen, who as captain of the *Trident* had recently torpedoed *Prinz Eugen*, and Commander W. R. Fell.

The other and more ambitious submersible was the midget submarine or X-craft, the brainchild of a retired submariner called Commander Cromwell Varley. It had a longer pedigree than the chariot, being similar to a conventional submarine, only smaller. It was 51 feet long, 6 feet in diameter, and had a diving depth of 300 feet. Instead of torpedoes, it carried side-charges containing two tons of amatex explosive. It was Varley's friendship with a distinguished former submariner, Admiral Sir Max Horton, Flag Officer Submarines, coupled with Winston Churchill's enthusiasm for the unusual, that speeded the X-craft's development. X-3, the prototype, was launched in March 1942, and, with other craft expected off the stocks during the year, another training area in the west of Scotland was designated for them.

For both X-craft and chariots, the battleship *Tirpitz*, sitting snugly in her berth at Foettenfjord, was clearly a prime target. But before either craft could be given the opportunity to attack her, a most disturbing signal reached the British Admiralty. It was from the British naval attaché in Stockholm, Captain Henry Denham, and was dated 18 June.

MOST IMMEDIATE
Following is German plan for attack on next Russian convoy.
1. Air reconnaissance to locate eastbound convoy when it reaches Jan Mayen. Bombing attacks from bases in North Norway will then be made.
2. Pocket battleships and six destroyers will move to Altenfjord, and *Tirpitz* and *Hipper* to Narvik area, probably Bogen Fjord. Naval forces may be expected to operate from their anchorages once convoy has reached 5 degrees east. Simultaneous attacks when convoy on meridian of Bear Island by two surface groups supported by U-boats and aircraft. Graded A.3.

Captain Denham had a friend in Swedish naval intelligence sympathetic to Britain, who from time to time passed him vital information for the Royal Navy. The year before, thanks to this friend, Captain Denham had been the first to inform the Admiralty that *Bismarck* and *Prinz Eugen* were breaking out — news that enabled Tovey early on to marshal his forces against them.

Now a new source of information had come Denham's way. The German teleprinter lines to northern Norway ran partly through Sweden, and recently the Swedes had been able to crack the codes in which the signals were sent. The new information passed to Denham by his friend was a précis of the German fleet commander's signal to Group North of four days earlier for attacking the next Russian convoy. This intelligence — straight from the horse's mouth — Denham now passed to the Admiralty.

What new factors had emerged to counter Hitler's directive that *Tirpitz* was to be kept as a fleet-in-being, to enable the German naval staff to plan further operations against a Russian convoy?

Several things. First, and paradoxically, Hitler's insistence on the fleet being concentrated in Norway naturally spurred the naval staff to consider actions for it to perform. Secondly, Hitler had also insisted on an increase of U-boat strength in Norway, and these would provide a useful scouting force. Thirdly, Hitler had authorised a huge increase in air forces in northern Norway — more than 250 operational planes, which, in addition to their attacking role, would be invaluable for watching the movements of the convoys and the British fleet. Fourthly, after some lean months, there had been a new allocation of 15,000 tons of fuel oil for fleet operations for June.

The man who would direct the operation at sea was the fleet commander, the monkey-faced General-Admiral Otto Schniewind, recently Chief of Naval Operations. His broad plan was that the fleet should be divided into two battlegroups: the pocket battleships *Scheer* and

Lützow under Vice-Admiral Oskar Kummetz (who had lost his flagship *Blücher* in Oslo Fjord during the invasion of Norway) at Narvik, and *Tirpitz* and *Hipper* under himself at Trondheim. Overall control of the operation, as with PQ 12, would be in the hands of the bearded Admiral Carls of Naval Group North at Kiel. He would be in constant touch with Admiral Raeder in Berlin, who would in turn be in touch with Vice-Admiral Krancke (captain of *Scheer* on her 1940 raiding operations) at the Führer's headquarters.

As soon as the convoy was sighted, both battlegroups would proceed north, Schniewind's group to Vestfjord, Kummetz's to Altenfjord, where their destroyers would top up with fuel. Then, when the convoy was passing Bear Island, both groups would sail, rendezvous 100 miles north of the North Cape, descend on the convoy and annihilate it, and return at high speed to the fjords. The British battlefleet had never dared venture so far east, so the danger posed by their carriers would be negligible. Raeder flew to Trondheim to discuss the plans with Schniewind on 30 May and Carls himself came in early June. To all of them it seemed an operation in which they had every tactical advantage, which – unless Hitler got cold feet – promised to be the greatest German naval victory of the war.

The plans were put to Hitler, and he approved. His overjoyed admirals now waited for the sighting of convoy PQ 17.

When Admiral Pound read Denham's signal, he was deeply worried. He had lost two cruisers, *Edinburgh* and *Trinidad*, on recent Russian convoys; now the enormously valuable convoy, PQ 17, was about to sail, and here was a formidable force preparing to attack it. Later he put through a call to Tovey to express his fears; he himself would have cancelled PQ 17, but the politicians had insisted on it. He told Tovey that if at any moment he thought the convoy was facing annihilation, he might possibly order it to scatter. Tovey was horrified; all his own experience told him that a convoy that kept formation was the best defence against whatever might attack it. If such an order was given, he told Pound, the result would be 'sheer, bloody murder'.

Before long, events were to prove him right.

4. PQ 17

Since the abortive PQ 12 operation, life on board *Tirpitz* in Foettenfjord had resumed its customary harbour routine. Under the lee of the high hill, unaware that the eyes of Rörholt, Grönn and others were on them, the crew went about their daily duties of cleaning and storing ship. Occasionally there were trips down the fjord for exercises, which gave them a welcome change of scene. Even the air raids came as a gratifying diversion, for they involved them in the war, proved, too, the efficiency of the ship's defensive system.

The twenty-second of March was Wehrmacht Day, and the crew collected 81,000 marks for Winter Relief, more than double the previous year. At a ceremony to present this money to the captain, the crew's spokesman said, 'Captain, sir, in handing you this money, we make one condition.'

'Oh,' said Topp, 'and what is that?'

'That you grow a beard.'

The captain's views about beards were well known, yet how could he refuse, knowing the fun it would give the crew?

'Very well,' he said, and the crew cheered. And Charlie Topp grew a beard, so rich and luxuriant that when a month later Admiral Schniewind came on board he wondered for a moment who Topp was. Then, honour satisfied, Topp shaved it off.

The days grew longer and the nights warmer. The snow began to melt on the slopes, and instead of ski-ing there was fishing in the lakes and streams, walks among the woods and hills. Two miles from the ship, at the entrance to Foettenfjord, there was an island called Salto, with holiday cabins on it, pine trees, grassy fields, wild flowers. Captain Topp obtained permission from the Trondheim Kommandatur to requisition it as a leave centre, and called it Tipito.

Here small groups of men from each of the ship's twelve divisions were allowed to stay for three or four days at a time. They cleaned and painted the holiday cabins, called them after ships' officers with such names as the Düwelsberg, the Kumpelwiese, the Rovenichhaus; the officers' house was known as the Perrigheim after Lieutenant Perrig, the camouflage officer, who repainted it. An open-air theatre was put up, and on the day Tipito opened there was a concert by *Tirpitz*'s band.

German correctness ensured that the rules at Tipito were strict. There was to be no hunting, no picking of plants or flowers, no camp fires, no taking of eggs – and above all no invitations to Norwegians to visit the island as guests. But when there are deals to be made, rules are conveniently forgotten. From the Germans the Norwegians wanted alcohol and tobacco; from the Norwegians the Germans wanted fresh vegetables and eggs; and a barter system was arranged to mutual satisfaction.

There was something else the Germans wanted too – girls – so for Tipito parties local girls were discreetly ferried out, both to officers and men. This happy state of affairs might have continued indefinitely had not a Norwegian boatman had to stand trial for stealing food from Tipito stores. To get his own back he gave evidence of carrying girls to and from the island. For this breach of discipline the Trondheim Kommandatur closed Tipito down.

But the men of *Tirpitz* did not have to lament its passing for long. On 1 July the Luftwaffe first sighted PQ 17, east of Jan Mayen Island, and next day Admiral Schniewind signalled ships in company: 'From Fleet Commander. To *Tirpitz*, *Hipper* and destroyers. Raise steam for 25 knots and be ready to proceed by 1600 today 2nd. Acknowledge.'

Operation RÖSSELSPRUNG ('Knight's Move') had begun.

On the afternoon of 27 June the thirty-five merchant ships that were to comprise convoy PQ 17 steamed in line ahead out of the anchorage at Hvalfjord, Iceland, and once in the open sea took up their appointed positions in nine columns. It was one of the most valuable convoys ever to put to sea, worth, at one estimate, over £200 million. It was carrying nearly 300 aircraft, 600 tanks, more than 4000 lorries and carriers, over 150,000 tons of general cargo – enough to equip a Russian army of 50,000 men. For its close escort it had fourteen screening vessels, under Commander Jack Broome in the destroyer *Keppel*; there was also a covering force of four cruisers, *London*, *Norfolk* and the Americans *Wichita* and *Tuscaloosa*, with three destroyers, under the command of Rear-Admiral 'Turtle' Hamilton; and in distant support was the British battlefleet consisting of the *Duke of York*, the American battleship *Washington*, the carrier *Victorious*, two cruisers and fourteen destroyers under Admiral Sir John Tovey.

No one on board the merchantmen and warships had any illusions about the dangers of the journey that faced them. They knew of the long hours of daylight that lay ahead, that *Scheer* and *Lützow* were at Narvik, that *Tirpitz* might be sailed to join them. An American naval officer in the cruiser *Wichita*, Lieutenant Douglas Fairbanks, Jr, observing the merchant ships 'waddle out to sea like so many dirty ducks', wrote in his diary, 'Everyone who was watching them paid a silent tribute and offered some half-thought prayer.' His commanding officer, Captain Hill, had few doubts that they would see action. To a group of officers after dinner he said, 'All my life I've been studying, training and waiting for this moment – and now it's come. Good luck to you all.'

For the next four days the convoy, surrounded by its escort vessels, steamed north-eastwards at 9 knots. The sea was calm and the weather misty, which prevented the Luftwaffe from sighting them. It wasn't until the afternoon of 1 July that first a Focke-Wulf reconnaissance plane and then the U-boat U-456, part of a long patrol line, sighted it. From this moment U-boats and aircraft remained in touch almost continuously.

But the Germans took their time about attacking. More than twenty-four hours went by before they launched a strike of seven Heinkel He 115 torpedo-bombers. These came in from the south-east at 6.30 on the evening of 2 July. They scored no hits, and one of them was shot down.

At 8 p.m. that evening, as the unsuccessful Heinkels were returning to Bödö, *Tirpitz*, *Hipper* and four destroyers were heading down Trondheimsfjord for the open sea. Schniewind had hoped to sail the day before, when the convoy was first sighted, but Hitler was in East Prussia and Raeder had insisted on getting his approval. Despite this delay everyone on board, from Schniewind down to the youngest able seaman, was in exalted mood, for all believed, and with reason, that they were on the verge of a great victory.

Through the thickening mist the squadron negotiated the tortuous Naröy Sound, Topp spurning the services of a tug that had been standing by, as confident of his brilliant seamanship as ever. Going out against PQ 12 in March he had taken the advice of the Norwegian pilot in avoiding Vegas Fjord: today, because he knew Schniewind was in a hurry, he cut through it without difficulty. Only once on the run north, between Kaura and Grinna, did he have to leave the inner leads; he made the passage at 25 knots and was back in sheltered waters within the hour. He and Commander Bidlingmaier, the navigator, were a remarkably cool pair.

Next morning the squadron was running up Vestfjord to an anchorage at Gimsöy near Narvik. But on passing in line ahead through the Gimsöy narrows, three of the four destroyers, *Hans Lody, Karl Galster* and *Theodor Riedel*, struck an uncharted rock. The rest of the force came to anchor. The remaining destroyer, the *Friedrich Ihn*, was ordered to top up with fuel and be ready to sail in the evening.

The second battlegroup meanwhile – *Lützow, Scheer* and six destroyers under Admiral Kummetz – had left Narvik after midnight bound for Altenfjord. Nosing her way through the narrow Tjeld Sound in a thick fog, *Lützow* also ran into a rock, and so could take no further part in the operation. *Scheer* and the destroyers dropped anchor in Altenfjord at 10 a.m.

Tirpitz remained in Gimsöy only four hours, for by now Schniewind was desperate to get the operation started – indeed he could not understand why he had not received the executive order already. At 5.15 he sent *Tirpitz*'s Arado to Narvik with a message for Admiral Schmundt, commanding Northern Waters; this was to pass word by teleprinter to Admiral Carls that he proposed to sail with both battlegroups against the convoy next morning. Schmundt was appalled, knowing the executive order for RÖSSELSPRUNG had not been given. He suppressed the signal and telephoned Carls to say why. Carls approved and signalled Schniewind, 'Transfer to Altenfjord. Request intentions.'

By the time the impatient Schniewind received this, he had already given orders to sail on his own initiative and with *Hipper* and three destroyers was proceeding down Vestfjord at high speed. He replied that he was obeying instructions to proceed to Altenfjord, and hoped that the operation could be initiated the following morning.

At 10.30 a.m. next day the *Tirpitz* force joined *Scheer* and her destroyers in Altenfjord. Now all the frustrated Schniewind and Kummetz could do was wait, with their ships at the ready, for Admiral Carls to send them the order to sail.

Meanwhile the convoy was plodding east through a

glassy sea which made it impossible for the shadowing U-boats to attack. In the early morning of 4 July aircraft could be heard buzzing about in the low cloud, but only one broke through, and gliding down with its engines cut successfully torpedoed the merchant ship *Christopher Newport*, which fell astern and had to be abandoned.

For the rest of the day the ships maintained steady progress to the north-eastwards. By mid-morning, at about the time that Schniewind was joining Kummetz in Altenfjord, the convoy was directly north of the North Cape, already to the east of Bear Island. Morale was high and increased further when in the course of the morning Admiral Hamilton's cruiser force, which had been keeping out of sight to the northward, swept into sight ahead. Earlier Hamilton had sent Captain Hill of the *Wichita* congratulations on American Independence Day. Hill had replied, 'Independence Day always requires large fireworks. I trust you will not disappoint us.'

As the day wore on, it was clear that the fireworks would not long be delayed. From about 3 p.m. the convoy's radio operators were picking up almost continuous homing beacons from U-boats and aircraft in contact with the convoy. At 4.45 p.m. Commander Broome signalled his escorts to close the convoy at speed to give air support. A few minutes later the escorts hoisted Flag Q – air attack imminent.

The aircraft of this first wave were Heinkel He 115 torpedo-bombers of German Coastal Command, but they failed to press home their attack. For two hours they circled the convoy, trying to penetrate the screen, but each time a furious fire from the escort vessels succeeded in driving them back. In the end many dropped their torpedoes outside effective range.

There was a pause in the proceedings between 7 and 8 p.m., when crews were able to snatch something to eat and drink, then at 8.15 the second wave arrived. This consisted, first, of some Ju 88 bombers, which were soon driven off by accurate anti-aircraft fire, then of twenty-five Heinkel He 115 torpedo-bombers from the airfield at Bardufoss. These split into two groups, one coming in on the starboard bow of the convoy, the other on the starboard quarter.

The attack on the bow was largely foiled by the American destroyer *Wainwright*, which had left Hamilton's force to oil from a tanker in the convoy. She steered at 32 knots towards where the Heinkels were grouping, and met them with a hail of fire some 4000 yards from the convoy. One of the aircraft was shot down, and none of the torpedoes found their mark.

The attack on the starboard quarter was more successful. Despite a curtain of fire several aircraft pressed home their attacks, and launched at least twenty torpedoes. Some of these were deflected by small weapons fire while en route to their target, but three struck home, on the Russian tanker *Azerbaijan*, and the merchantmen *Navarino* and *William Hooper*. One of the Heinkels was shot down. The *Azerbaijan* later rejoined the convoy and eventually reached port, but the other two ships were lost.

Throughout the attacks – and indeed throughout the long tense hours before the attacks – morale remained wonderfully high. When the firing was at its height, the captain of one of the escorting submarines had signalled to Broome, 'Can I go home to Mum?', while the captain of an anti-submarine trawler had asked his neighbour, 'Are you happy in the service?' Now that the enemy had been beaten off there was a tremendous feeling of pride and achievement. Together, convoy and escorts could accomplish anything; there were only 800 miles to go now to journey's end, and danger of further attacks must recede with every passing hour.

And then out of the blue came a bombshell, or rather three bombshells, from the Admiralty in London.

The first, timed 9.11 p.m., said, 'Secret. Most Immediate. Cruiser force withdraw to westwards at high speed.' The second, at 9.23 p.m., said, 'Secret. Immediate. Owing to threat from surface ships, convoy is to disperse and proceed to Russian ports.' And the third, timed 9.36 p.m., said 'Secret. Most Immediate. Convoy is to scatter.'

On the bridges of Hamilton's cruisers and Broome's escorts, men looked at each other in dismay and bewilderment. This tight, brave, disciplined convoy to *scatter*? Why? The only possible reason could be that the Admiralty knew something they didn't know, i.e. that *Tirpitz* was on her way to attack them, at that very moment might be just below the southern horizon. Officers lifted their binoculars and peered in the direction of Norway. The horizon was blank.

'And then suddenly out of the blue came this signal to scatter, which shook us all to the core. We'd got no reason to believe there was anything to scatter about, but this could only mean one thing, that Tirpitz *was here, she was on the horizon. Up went all our glasses, and I remember expecting someone to say, there she is, there's a gun-flash, something like that.*

'I hoisted the signal to scatter, there was nothing else for me to do, it was an order from the Admiralty. As soon as I'd hoisted it, I looked round to the Commodore, he didn't seem to be repeating it. So I thought, well, there's no time to lose, she might be on us, and I shot into the convoy in Keppel, *went alongside the Commodore and switched on my loud-hailer. I saw the Commodore standing in the wing of the bridge, and I told him about scattering and he simply couldn't believe it. You see, we'd just been through the air attack, we'd done jolly well, everybody was on their toes and full of beans, and there was this sudden signal. Look, I said, this is true, and he sort of came to and he finally hoisted the signal. I said, I'm sorry about this, it looks like being a bloody business, and he said something like good-bye and good hunting.*

'So then I turned away and picked up the rest of my destroyers. And there was no doubt about it, they were all feeling the same as I was. Going on an opposite course to this

The fateful signals regarding PQ 17 as set out in Appendix II of the report of Rear Admiral Hamilton, commanding the First Cruiser Squadron, to Admiral Tovey, C.-in-C. Home Fleet.

1 To: C-in-C H.F. (R) ADMIRALTY 275
  From: C.S. ONE.

  SECRET. IMMEDIATE.

  Convoy position at 1200Z 075 deg. 25′ North, 024 deg. 20′ East. It is proceeding to 400 mile radius from Banak. Only casualty CHRISTOPHER NEWPORT torpedoed by aircraft and sunk by own forces.

  2. First Cruiser Squadron remaining in vicinity until enemy surface situation clarifies but certainly not repetition not later than 1200Z/5th July.

  T.O.O. = 1520B/4th July.

2 To: C.S. ONE (R) ADMIRALTY 764
  From: C-in-C H.F.

  SECRET. IMMEDIATE.

  Reference Admiralty's 1230/4.
  Once the convoy is to the Eastward of 025 degrees East or earlier at your discretion you are to leave the Barents Sea unless assured by Admiralty that TIRPITZ cannot be met.

  My position at 1500B/4 075 deg. 46′ North 010 deg. 40′ East, course 332 deg., altering at 1600B to south-westwards.

  T.O.O. = 1512B/4th July.

3 To: C-in-C H.F. (R) ADMIRALTY 276.
  From: C.S. ONE.

  SECRET. IMMEDIATE.

  Your 1512B/4
  Intend withdrawing to Westward about 2200B/4 on completion of Destroyer oiling.

  T.O.O. = 1809B/4th July.

In the early evening of 4 July the Admiralty were informed by Bletchley Park that the German naval codes for the 24-hour period ending at noon that day had been broken. As a result they shortly expected 'further information' about the movements of the German fleet. Until this arrived Admiral Hamilton's cruisers were to remain with the convoy.

4 To: C.S. ONE 59, (R) C-in-C H.F. 106.
  From: ADMIRALTY.

        SECRET. MOST IMMEDIATE.

        C.-in-C., H.F.'s 1512/4th and your 1520/4th.
        Further information may be available shortly.
        Remain with convoy pending further instructions.

        T.O.O. = 1858B/4th July.

Two hours later the decrypted signal from Naval Group North announcing *Tirpitz*'s expected arrival in Altenfjord that morning reached the Admiralty (see page 62) and as a result Admiral Pound ordered Admiral Hamilton's cruisers to withdraw at high speed, and the convoy to scatter.

5 To: C.S. ONE 65(R) C-in-C H.F. 114,
          H.F. OPERATIONAL.
  From: ADMIRALTY.

        SECRET. MOST IMMEDIATE.

        Cruiser Force withdraw to Westward at high speed.

        T.O.O. = 2111B/4th July.

6 To: ESCORT OF PQ17 (R) C.S. ONE 67, C-in-C. H.F.
          116.
  From: ADMIRALTY.

        SECRET. IMMEDIATE.

        Owing to threat from surface ships convoy is to
        disperse and proceed to Russian ports.

        T.O.O. = 2123/4th July.

7 To: ESCORT OF PQ17, (R) C-in-C. H.F. 117, C.S.
          ONE 68, H.F. OPERATIONAL.
  From: ADMIRALTY.

        SECRET. MOST IMMEDIATE.

        My 2123/4th. Convoy is to scatter.

        T.O.O. = 2136B/4th July.

scattering convoy, ships we were supposed to be looking after, going the other way, watching them get smaller on the horizon, that was terrible.'

Extract from Captain·Broome's interview on the BBC documentary programme, 'Target Tirpitz'.

What had led to this extraordinary decision, one that by its very nature was bound to condemn to death many of the convoy's merchantmen?

For the past forty-eight hours the Admiralty had been deeply worried about the whereabouts of *Tirpitz*. The day before (the 3rd), first aircraft reconnaissance, then an Ultra intercept had revealed that she had left her berth at Foettenfjord, but since then there had been no news of her. However, another Ultra intercept had brought intelligence that *Scheer* and her group had anchored in Altenfjord. Would *Tirpitz* join them?

The night of the 3rd and most of the 4th went by without any further news. Then, on the evening of the 4th, word came from Bletchley Park that the cryptographers had just broken the German naval cipher settings for the 24-hour period ending at noon that day; and from this came the news that *Tirpitz* and *Hipper* had been due to enter Altenfjord that morning. Furthermore, their destroyers had been ordered to top up with fuel.

With a pair of dividers and a chart, it did not take Admiral Pound long to work out that if the German ships had sailed, say, a couple of hours after reaching Altenfjord, they would, steaming at 28 knots, be in a position to reach the convoy any time after 2 a.m. on the 5th –i.e. in some six hours' time. And if that happened, thought Pound, the German ships, with superior speed, firepower and gun range, could annihilate the convoy and close escort, and severely damage Admiral Hamilton's cruisers.

But had *Tirpitz* sailed? The man who could best answer

that question was Paymaster Commander Norman Denning, chief intelligence officer for German main surface units. To his office Pound now repaired.

Denning held the view, based on some experience, that *Tirpitz* had not sailed. Firstly, the monitoring stations had not picked up any signals to her from Group North, which they certainly would have done if she had left harbour; secondly, the decrypted signals from Admiral Schmundt to the U-boats shadowing the convoy had contained no warning to look out for German surface ships; thirdly, our own submarines, waiting off the approaches to Altenfjord, would almost certainly have reported by radio the sailing of the German ships; and fourthly, the Norwegian radio agent who operated at the entrance to Altenfjord had not reported any enemy movements.

Unfortunately Pound did not ask Denning for these detailed reasons, and Denning, a junior officer, did not think it his place to volunteer them. 'Can you assure me,' Pound asked him, 'that *Tirpitz* is still at anchor in Altenfjord?' But Denning could not do this, as he would only have firm news after she had left. He hoped, however, he told Pound, to give him absolute assurance that she had not sailed as soon as Bletchley had broken the ciphers for the period starting at noon that day; and that this should be within the next three or four hours.

At 8 p.m. that evening Pound called a meeting of the naval operations staff, some dozen officers in all. In turn he asked each of them what line of action they recommended for the convoy in the face of the latest intelligence. Vice-Admiral Moore, Vice Chief of the Naval Staff, said that if it was to be dispersed, it should be done immediately, as the greater the delay the less sea-room for dispersal because of the ice. All other officers present said they did not recommend dispersal at the present time.

Admiral Pound then closed his eyes, so that one officer

The crucial Ultra signal that led Admiral Pound, the First Sea Lord, to order PQ 17 to scatter. It was sent early on the morning of 4 July from Admiral Schniewind, then approaching Alta with *Tirpitz* and *Hipper*, to Admiral Kummetz who had already reached Alta with *Scheer* and destroyers.

The decrypted message reached the Admiralty in the evening. Aware of the false reports contained in the previous Ultra signals (see page 70) of a battleship and carrier near the convoy, but unaware of Hitler's restrictions in relation to them, Pound concluded that having arrived at Alta at 9 a.m., the whole force must have put to sea immediately after oiling, and must now be closing the convoy at high speed. Hence the order to scatter.

The decision was taken against the advice not only of the rest of the Naval staff, but of the chief intelligence officer, Paymaster Commander Norman Denning, who assured Pound that he would know very soon after the enemy had sailed because of wireless traffic addressed to them from Naval Group North, Admiral Commanding Northern Waters, etc. Pound was unimpressed.

4 July 1942

TOO   0740

FROM: C IN C FLEET

TO: ADMIRAL COMMANDING CRUISERS

IMMEDIATE

ARRIVING ALTA 0900. YOU ARE TO ALLOT ANCHORAGES TIRPITZ OUTER VAGFJORD (AS RECEIVED). NEWLY ARRIVING DESTROYERS AND TORPEDO BOATS TO COMPLETE WITH FUEL AT ONCE.

It was this Ultra signal, received at the Admiralty very soon after Admiral Pound had given the order for PQ 17 to scatter on the evening of 4 July, that led Paymaster Commander Denning to ask his superior Admiral Clayton to try and persuade Pound to cancel it. The firm information given to the Eisteufel group of U-boats round the convoy that none of their own naval forces were in the operational area, coupled with the continued lack of any wireless traffic to *Tirpitz*, were proof to Denning that the force had not sailed. But Pound refused to budge.

TOO   1130

FROM: ADMIRAL COMMANDING NORTHERN WATERS

TO: EISTEUFEL

NO OWN NAVAL FORCES IN THE OPERATIONAL AREA. POSITION OF HEAVY ENEMY GROUP NOT KNOWN AT PRESENT, BUT IS THE MAJOR TARGET FOR U-BOATS WHEN ENCOUNTERED. BOATS IN CONTACT WITH THE CONVOY ARE TO KEEP AT IT. NO AIRCRAFT IN CONTACT WITH THE CONVOY AT THE MOMENT. RECONNAISSANCE IS BEING OPERATED.

present thought he had fallen asleep. In fact he was thinking, and what he may well have been thinking was that every forecast of early enemy movements contained in Captain Denham's signal of 18 June – air reconnaissance on the convoy, then air attack, the move to Altenfjord by the pocket battleships, the move to Narvik by *Tirpitz* and *Hipper* – had been fulfilled to the letter. What possible reason was there to doubt that the last part of the signal, 'simultaneous attacks by two surface groups supported by U-boats and aircraft when on the meridian of Bear Island', would not be fulfilled also?

Admiral Pound knew what he was going to do – indeed it might be said he had known it for days. A week earlier he had approved the convoy sailing orders which had contained this pregnant last paragraph: 'Once convoy is to eastwards of meridian of Bear Island circumstances may arise in which best thing would be for convoy to be dispersed with orders to proceed to Russian ports.' He had expressed the same thoughts in his recent telephone conversation with Tovey. And only that morning he had asked an officer in the Admiralty Trade Division whether, if the convoy was scattered, it would still be possible to communicate with each ship in code.

At last Pound opened his eyes.

'The convoy is to disperse,' he said.

When Denning's superior, Admiral Clayton, brought him this news, Denning was greatly depressed. A long time now had gone by without any signals from Group North to *Tirpitz*, a sure sign that she was still in Altenfjord (where she would receive signals overland); and to confirm this, a decrypted signal had just come in from Admiral Schmundt at Narvik informing the U-boats round the convoy that German surface units were not operating in their area.

In the light of this Denning persuaded Clayton to go back to Pound and try and persuade him to change his mind. With great moral courage Clayton did so. But he

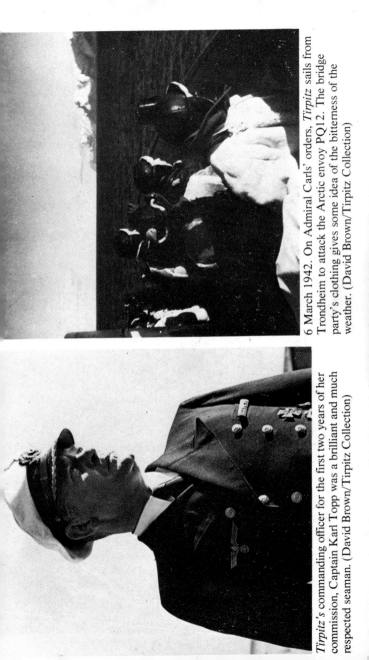

Tirpitz's commanding officer for the first two years of her commission, Captain Karl Topp was a brilliant and much respected seaman. (David Brown/Tirpitz Collection)

6 March 1942. On Admiral Carls' orders, *Tirpitz* sails from Trondheim to attack the Arctic envoy PQ12. The bridge party's clothing gives some idea of the bitterness of the weather. (David Brown/Tirpitz Collection)

January 1942. Her long training in the Baltic over, Tirpitz becomes operational at last as she sails from Kiel to her war station in Norway. (David Brown/Tirpitz Collection)

Painting swastikas to be placed on deck for German aircraft recognition. (David Brown/Tirpitz Collection)

Tirpitz at speed. She had an advantage of some two knots over any British battleship. (David Brown/Tirpitz Collection)

A reconnaissance plane from *Victorious* sights the *Tirpitz* and *Friedrich hn* west of the Lofoten Islands on their return passage to Trondheim. David Brown/Crown Copyright)

5 July 1942. After much hesitation and long delay the German fleet is at last given permission to sail to attack PQ 17. *Tirpitz* (foreground), *Hipper*, *Lützow* and destroyers head for the open sea. (John MacClancy Press Ltd/U.S. Navy)

Convoy PQ 17 is sighted by the Luftwaffe. (David Brown/Tirpitz Collection)

Admiral Sir John Tovey, Commander-in-Chief, British Home Fleet. In May 1941 the guns of his flagship *King George V* sank the *Bismarck*. The Home Fleet gave cover to convoy PQ 17.

Admiral of the Fleet Sir Dudley Pound, British First Sea Lord. His signal to PQ 17 to scatter resulted in one of the greatest British naval disasters of the war. (Imperial War Museum)

4 July 1942. With anti-aircraft guns at the ready *Tirpitz* waits in Altenfjord for the signal to sail against PQ 17. (David Brown/Tirpitz Collection)

Tirpitz (foreground), *Lützow* and *Hipper* in Altenfjord, still waiting for the signal to sail. (David Brown/Tirpitz Collection)

The two-man crew of a chariot under way in a Scottish sea loch.
(Submarine Museum, Gosport)

An X-craft or midget submarine under way. (Keystone)

Captain Topp and Admiral Schneiwind on the bridge of *Tirpitz* during her brief sortie against *PQ 17*. (David Brown/Tirpitz Collection)

Grand Admiral Erich Raeder, Supreme Commander of the German Navy for fourteen years. (Imperial War Museum)

was unsuccessful. The signal had been sent, said Pound, and was probably now being acted on; in any case the matter had been decided.

And so, 2000 miles away, Commander Broome had the unenviable task of confirming the order to scatter to an astonished convoy commodore (so astonished he asked for it to be repeated); and then, before the eyes of all those merchant sailors whose ships it had been his duty to protect, of collecting his destroyers together, joining Hamilton's retreating cruisers, and abandoning the merchant ships to their fate. 'It was such a terrible feeling,' wrote Douglas Fairbanks in *Wichita*, 'to be running away from the convoy at a speed twice theirs, and to leave them to the mercies of the enemy.'

Such was the effect of Pound's order to scatter.

On the night of 4 July, when Hamilton and his cruisers, recently joined by Broome and his destroyers, were withdrawing at high speed to the westward, and the ships of the convoy were fanning outwards to scatter, all in the belief that *Tirpitz* and her consorts were about to overwhelm them, where was the German fleet? Lying at anchor in Altenfjord, where it had been all day. For more than twelve hours Schniewind and Kummetz, beside themselves with frustration, had been waiting for orders to sail that never came. What had gone wrong?

Many things. Firstly, during the night before, when *Tirpitz* and *Hipper* were on passage from Bogen to Altenfjord, a Luftwaffe pilot had sighted Hamilton's force and wrongly reported that it included a battleship as well as cruisers. Until this could be confirmed, *Tirpitz* had to remain in harbour, as Hitler had directed that she was not to engage enemy battleships. Next morning another plane correctly identified Hamilton's force as consisting only of cruisers and destroyers, but around lunchtime Lieutenant-Commander Brandenburg in U-457 repeated the first aircraft's error in reporting a battleship among Hamilton's force. Then, at 6.30 p.m.,

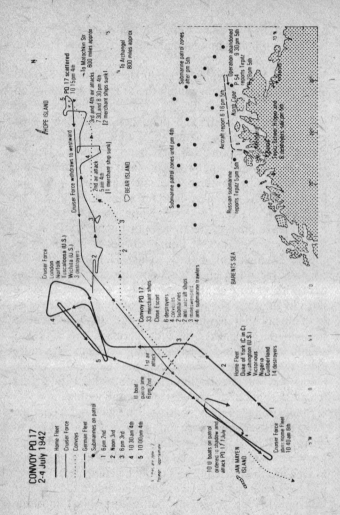

CONVOY PQ 17
2-4 July 1942

— Home Fleet
---- Cruiser Force
········ Convoys
—·— German Fleet

● Submarines on patrol
1 6pm 2nd
2 Noon 3rd
3 6pm 3rd
4 10.30am 4th
5 10.00pm 4th

JAN MAYEN
ISLAND

10 U boats on patrol
ordered to shadow and
attack PQ 17 1 July

Cruiser Force
parts company
10.40am 6th

Home Fleet
Duke of York (C in C)
Washington (U.S.)
Victorious
Nigeria
Cumberland
14 destroyers

U boat
patrol line
6pm 2nd

1st air
attack

Cruiser Force
London
Norfolk
Tuscaloosa (U.S.)
Wichita (U.S.)
3 destroyers

Convoy PQ 17
33 merchant ships
Close Escort
6 destroyers
4 corvettes
2 submarines
2 anti-aircraft ships
3 minesweepers
4 anti-submarine trawlers

Cruiser Force withdraws to westward

2nd air attack
5 am 4th
[1 merchant ship sunk]

3rd and 4th air attacks
7.30 and 8.30 pm 4th
[2 merchant ships sunk]

PQ 17 scattered
10 15pm 4th

To Matochkin Str
600 miles approx

To Archangel
800 miles approx

HOPE ISLAND

BEAR ISLAND

BARENTS SEA

Submarine patrol zones until 4th

Submarine patrol zones
after pm 5th

Aircraft report 6 16pm 5th

North Cape

Russian submarine
reports 1 year 2 5pm 5th

Tirpitz Scheer Hipper and
6 destroyers sail 3 00pm 5th

Operation abandoned
9 30pm 5th

N

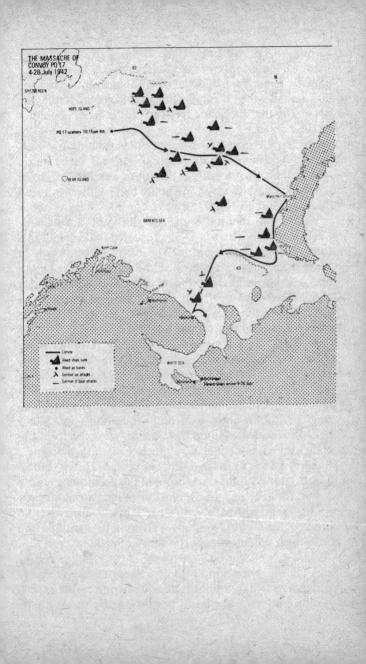

THE MASSACRE OF
CONVOY PQ 17
4-28 July 1942

ICE

N

SPITZBERGEN

HOPE ISLAND

PQ 17 scatters 10.15pm 4th

BEAR ISLAND

BARENTS SEA

Matochkin Strait

North Cape

ICE

WHITE SEA

Convoy
Allied ships sunk
Allied air bases
German air attacks
German U-boat attacks

to add to the worries of the naval staff, an aircraft shadowing the convoy reported having seen 'two torpedo planes'. These were *Wichita*'s float-planes sent up to keep down shadowing U-boats, but to Raeder in Berlin the possibility that they were from a British carrier could not be discounted.

For the German fleet time was now running out fast. On the evening of the 5th Admiral Carls informed Berlin that if the order for RÖSSELSPRUNG was not approved within the next twenty-four hours he proposed to recall the battlefleet to Narvik. Raeder agreed. Then, at about midnight on the night of the 4th–5th, Lieutenant-Commander Teichert in U-456 reported that Hamilton's force was withdrawing at high speed to the westward. In the light of this Carls proposed to Raeder that the battle-fleet should sail at once. But to no avail: the British Home Fleet had not been sighted for some time, and Hitler's directive that *Tirpitz* was not to attack until its carrier had been neutralised was still in force.

At 6.55 a.m., however, a Luftwaffe reconnaissance plane made a chance sighting of the Home Fleet, including the carrier *Victorious*, 200 miles north-west of Bear Island and steering south-west; this was some 800 miles from where the German ships would attack the convoy. Surely now, with both Hamilton's imaginary battleship and the Home Fleet carrier removed from the scene, the attack could take place. Carls asked Raeder, Raeder asked Krancke, Krancke asked Hitler, Hitler approved. At 9 a.m. Carls brought the fleet to one hour's notice for sea, and at 11 a.m. to immediate notice; at 11.30, having finally received Hitler's blessing, he ordered Schniewind to sail. Yet even he qualified the order with a depressingly restrictive telegram:

A brief operation with partial success is more important than a total victory involving major expenditure of time. Report at once if overflown by enemy aircraft. Do not hesitate to break off operation if situation doubtful. On no account grant enemy success against fleet nucleus.

It would be difficult to think of a more pusillanimous directive, in sharp contrast to the British Navy's traditional exhortations of 'Engage the enemy more closely' and 'Sink, burn and destroy. Let nothing pass.'

By the time the frustrated Schniewind had received his sailing orders, he had already anticipated them, and with his whole force was steaming down the leads to the open sea. Signals of successes by U-boats and aircraft against the convoy had been arriving in the fleet during the past twenty-four hours, and officers and men hoped there would still be a slice of the action left for them. Schniewind chose the western Rolvsöy exit rather than going by Nordkinn, as Carls had ordered, and by 3 p.m. his force, steaming at 25 knots, was heading east-north-east into the Barents Sea.

But if Schniewind had hoped to approach the convoy unobserved, he was in for a shock. Two hours after clearing the coast he was sighted by Commander Lunin in the Russian submarine K-21, who fired torpedoes at *Tirpitz*, claiming, wrongly, two hits. An hour later the force was sighted by a patrolling British aircraft from Murmansk, and again two hours later by the British submarine P-54.

These sighting reports were picked up by the German monitoring service, and at Kiel and in Berlin caused some anxiety. Perhaps the British fleet, on receiving Lunin's report, had at once reversed course and was even now steaming eastwards with its carrier to cut off the German ships from their base. The possibility was remote, yet remained a possibility. Taken in conjunction with the reports that had been flowing in all day of U-boats and aircraft sinking individual ships of the convoy, and the fact that the convoy as a unit had almost ceased to exist,

THREE ULTRA SIGNALS THAT EXPLAIN THE HESITANCY OF THE GERMAN NAVAL HIGH COMMAND IN COMMITTING THE *TIRPITZ* FORCE AGAINST PQ 17 IN THE LIGHT OF HITLER'S RESTRICTIVE ORDERS ABOUT ENEMY CARRIERS AND BATTLESHIPS.

1. Lieutenant-Commander Brandenburg in U-457 wrongly reports an enemy battleship in Admiral Hamilton's cruiser force.

2. Luftwaffe shadower C 3/406 wrongly reports an enemy battleship in Admiral Hamilton's cruiser force.

3. U-boats shadowing convoy (codenamed 'Eisteufel Group') given wrong Luftwaffe assumption that an enemy carrier is in the vicinity. The plane spotted near the convoy came not from a carrier but the American cruiser *Wichita*.

3 July 1942

1. TOO   1625

    FROM: BRANDENBURG

    MOST IMMEDIATE

    FORCES REPORTED ARE 1 BATTLESHIP, 2 CRUISERS, 3 DESTROYERS IN SQUARE 1542 LEFT CENTRE. COURSE 130 DEGREES. MODERATE SPEED.

---

4 July

2. TOO   0040

    FROM: FLIEGERFUEHRER LOFOTEN

    TO: ALL

    MOST IMMEDIATE

    OWN SHADOWER 'C' 3/406 REPORTS AT 0015: AM IN CONTACT WITH 1 BATTLESHIP, 1 HEAVY CRUISER, 2 LIGHT CRUISERS, 3 DESTROYERS, COURSE 060 DEGREES.

3. TOO   2344

   TO: EISTEUFEL

   LUFTWAFFE REPORTS: AT 2218 ONE HEAVY, TWO
   LIGHT CRUISERS WITH CONVOY. AT 2240 IN SQUARE
   AB 3943 ONE BATTLESHIP, THREE HEAVY CRUISERS,
   3 DESTROYERS, COURSE 300 DEGREES, 20 KNOTS. IT
   IS ASSUMED THAT THERE IS AN AIRCRAFT CARRIER
   IN THE AREA. SHADOWING AIRCRAFT IN CONTACT
   WITH CONVOY AND IS SENDING BEACON SIGNALS.

Raeder decided the operation was no longer worth the risks. At 9 p.m. he radioed to the fleet commander the single word *'Abbrechen'* ('Break off').

Lieutenant Edmund Kühnen was on watch on *Tirpitz*'s bridge when he saw a flag being hoisted from Schniewind's signal-deck above him.

'Red pennant,' said the signalman. 'Fleet to alter course 180 degrees.'

That meant turning round. Kühnen called Topp, Topp went up to Schniewind's bridge and came down looking glum.

'We're going back,' he said, 'Berlin's called it off.'

The executive signal came down, the ships turned from east to west. They reached Altenfjord in the small hours of the 6th, and in turn Admiral Kummetz, Captain Meisel of the *Hipper* and Commodore Bey in command of the destroyers came on board *Tirpitz* to propose that a smaller force of, say, the fastest destroyers, with or without *Hipper*, return to the Barents Sea to gather the pickings that remained. But the proposals were turned down, and at 6 p.m. that evening, with morale at a very low ebb, the German ships sailed for Narvik.

Meanwhile, out in the cold wastes of the Arctic, U-boats and Luftwaffe bombers completed the work of destruction they had begun the previous day. Of the thirty-five ships that had sailed with such high hopes from Hvalfjord, Iceland, on 27 June, only eleven finally reached Archangel in Russia.

Tirpitz had won a great victory without firing a shot.

For the British the massacre of PQ 17 and the abandoning of its charges by the Royal Navy was one of the most shameful episodes of the naval war. No wonder news of it was suppressed from the public until after hostilities had ended.

The responsibility for the débâcle inevitably lies with Admiral Pound, though less for his appreciation of the situation than for his response to it. He cannot be blamed for thinking that the German fleet had sailed. For what other reason had the two battlegroups concentrated in Altenfjord, the nearest anchorage to the convoy's route, and almost as exactly prophesied in Captain Denham's signal of 17 June?

He knew that *Tirpitz*, *Lützow*, *Scheer* and *Hipper* were more than a match for Hamilton's cruiser force, and that once the German ships had disposed of these and Broome's destroyers the convoy would be entirely at their mercy. He was not to know that *Lützow* had hit a rock and was out of the operation, nor of the false report that Hamilton's force included a battleship, nor of the crippling restrictions that Hitler had placed on the operations of his fleet. All he knew was what he, or any other British admiral, would have done in the circumstances – sail at once to attack and destroy the most tempting of targets.

But if Pound was justified in his appreciation, there can be no excuse for his panicky order, given against the advice of all but one of the naval staff, for the convoy to scatter. Denning had categorically stated that while he could not say for certain that the German ships were still in Altenfjord, he would know *within a few hours* of their leaving that they were at sea. It would have taken the German force twenty hours to reach the convoy, so there would have been plenty of time for the ships to scatter before the enemy arrived.

Admiral Pound was an officer prone to court-martialling or otherwise disciplining senior officers for what he considered to be errors of judgement. His own error of judgement in ordering PQ 17 to scatter was no less deserving of censure, yet his efforts to avoid it were contemptible. On 1 August he told the Cabinet that he had given the order to scatter because 'on the night of July 3rd–4th the Admiralty became possessed of intelligence that the *Tirpitz* had eluded our patrolling submarines and could be in a position to attack the convoy

73

on the morning of the 5th'. But in his official history Captain Roskill states that 'the existence of such precise intelligence has not been confirmed by post-war research'.

Little credit can go to the German Navy either for its part in the operation. It is true that as a result of the move north by the battlefleet two-thirds of the convoy was lost to U-boats and the Luftwaffe. But an even greater victory, the possible destruction of Hamilton's cruisers and destroyers as well as the convoy, had been there for the asking. Certainly there was a risk of some German ships being damaged in the process, but few operations of war have ever succeeded without risks. Had Hitler allowed his fleet commanders their head, not circumscribed them with restrictions at every turn, they might not only have gained a victory that would have done wonders for morale, but persuaded the British that sending war supplies to their enemy was no longer a sound operation of war.

Even as it was, after the arrival of the next convoy, PQ 18, which lost ten ships, all further sailings to Russia were suspended until the winter.

For the rest of the summer of 1942 *Tirpitz* remained at Bogen Bay, occasionally venturing into Vestfjord for exercises and coming to short notice for sea for three days in mid-August when it was thought, wrongly, that PQ 18 was en route to Russia. Schemes were devised to keep the men occupied – shopping trips to Narvik, excursions to the Swedish frontier – but with the nights as light as the day and no action or prospect of any, many of the crew felt frustrated and bored.

One morning the ship's muster was being taken.

'Schmitt!'

'Present.'

'Fitchel!'

'Present.'

'Turowski!'

No answer.

'Turowski!'

Still no answer. Turowski was an eighteen-year-old seaman, part of the crew of a flak gun. Inquiries were made: he hadn't been in the mess for supper the night before, and had last been seen during the previous afternoon. The ship was searched, but there was no sign of him.

Four days passed without news, then a car drew up on the jetty, and out of it came Turowski in civilian clothes, handcuffed to two military policemen. They had picked him up near the Swedish frontier, thirty miles away. He was armed with a revolver which he had stolen from an officer. He was taken before the officer of the watch, then consigned to one of the ship's cells, with a guard outside the door.

Two days later Captain Topp convened a court-martial in the main lecture-hall, consisting of half a dozen senior officers. Turowski was asked to account for himself. He was quite frank.

'I deserted,' he said, 'because I was bored. Nothing ever happens here.'

'Where did you intend to go?'

'When I reached Sweden, I hoped to go to Britain or America and join one of their merchant navies.'

The boy seemed unaware that he was writing his own death-warrant — a self-confessed deserter whose proclaimed intention was to go over to the enemy. The defending officer did his best, but there was little he could say. The sentence was a foregone conclusion: execution by firing squad.

The findings had to go to Admiral Carls at Kiel for approval. Topp, in forwarding the papers, asked that as a warning to others who might have the same idea sentence should be carried out on board. For six days Turowski remained in the cells, then the court-martial papers arrived from Kiel. Above Carls's signature and the stamp of Flag officer, Naval Group North, was the single word 'Approved'.

Next morning the ship's company, apart from those on duty, mustered on the quarter-deck. Turowski was brought up from the cells by two officers, led to a position abaft the after gun turret, and blindfolded. The firing squad, twelve of his messmates, fellow crewmen of the flak gun, were ordered to bring their rifles to the ready.

The chaplain, Pastor Muller, stepped forward and asked Turowski if he wished to say anything. Turowski shook his head but murmured to Muller, who had been good to him, *'Auf wiedersehen.'* Pastor Muller stepped back, the firing squad were ordered to raise their rifles.

'Fire!'

The shots echoed round the still fjord, Turowski's body fell to the deck. Despite his crime, there were few who saw him die who were not shocked: it was the enemy they ought to be killing, not their own people. *Tirpitz*, for some days afterwards, was less than a happy ship.

Turowski's body was taken to the military cemetery ashore, but two hours later brought back; the people at the cemetery refused to bury the body of a deserter and traitor. So four men were detailed to put Turowski's body in a weighted sack, place it in a boat, and dump it in the deepest part of the fjord.

By the end of August *Tirpitz* had been operational for over a year, and it was essential that she should undergo some kind of refit. Raeder would have liked her to dock in Germany, but Hitler refused to let her leave Norwegian waters. If she was not to be serviced in a proper dockyard, the best place to refit her in Norway was at her old berth in Foettenfjord.

She sailed there on 23 October, and two days later Admiral Sir Max Horton, Flag Officer Submarines, sent the following signal to a remote base in Shetland: 'Carry out Operation TITLE – target *Tirpitz* in Foettenfjord – D-Day, October 31st.'

5. The Chariots

Commanders Sladen and Fell had established their base for the chariots and X-craft at Fort Blockhouse, Portsmouth, in April, and soon after the first of the charioteers or, as the Admiralty called them, 'Volunteers for Hazardous Operations', arrived for training. Among the thirty-one volunteers were Sub-Lieutenant Jock Brewster, a Scot, Sergeant Craig of the Royal Engineers, Able Seaman Brown and Able Seaman Bob Evans. They underwent escapes in the 90-foot diving tank, practised riding dummy chariots in an experimental tank, then, when the operational chariots arrived, carried out exercises on them in a deserted part of Portsmouth harbour.

But in Portsmouth they could be seen, and as secrecy was essential a new base was established as far from habitation as possible – in the desolate Loch Erisort near Stornoway in the Hebrides. Here further prolonged exercises were carried out in conditions similar to those of the Norwegian fjords, and here Brewster, Craig, Brown and Evans learned that they had been chosen for an attack on the *Tirpitz*. Two other men, Able Seamen Billy Tebb and Malcolm Causer, were detailed to act as their dressers.

Now came the question as to how to transport the chariots to as near the target as possible. Obviously no warship or other large vessel would be able to penetrate far into German-controlled Norwegian waters; indeed the only vessel that stood any chance of bluffing its way past the shore batteries and guard-vessels was a local fishing-boat or trawler, of the kind that frequented these waters. But where to find one?

The only harbour in Britain in which such vessels were to be found was at Lunna Voe in the Shetland Islands, the headquarters of an extraordinary clandestine organisation nicknamed the 'Shetland Bus'. Here were based several Norwegian fishing-boats which had escaped from Norway since the occupation; their crews, under British supervision, were now running a two-way service to the Norwegian fjords, taking over agents, saboteurs, radio equipment and weapons, and bringing back returning agents, volunteers and refugees. It was one of these boats, the *Arthur*, skippered by Leif Larsen, that had taken Björn Rörholt to Trondheim. Now Larsen was asked if he would take two chariots and their crews over to attack the *Tirpitz*. He at once agreed.

But there was much to be done first. Once inside Norwegian waters the *Arthur* had to pass as a genuine local fishing-boat. What papers would she need to be cleared by the guard-boat that lay close to Agdenes, at the mouth of Trondheimsfjord? A Norwegian agent, Arne Christiansen, was sent from Sweden to Trondheim to find out. He contacted various resistance workers such as Rörholt's friend, Birger Grönn, manager of the dockyard, Herbert Helgesen, manager of a sausage factory and deliberately friendly with the Germans, Herluf Nygaard and others. From them he learned that the *Arthur* would require a cargo manifest, a certified crew list, ship's registration papers, identity cards for each of the crew, special permits to enter the Trondheim military zone, and a certificate signed by the various German harbourmasters of all the ports the *Arthur* had visited during the past three months. The resistance people promised to obtain sets of all these, and Helgesen also volunteered to obtain details of the nets surrounding the *Tirpitz* — these had been made in a local factory, whose manager he knew.

A month later another Norwegian agent, Odd Sörli, went to Trondheim from Sweden, collected the necessary papers and, disguised as a Norwegian pastor, brought them first to Stockholm, then to London. Here rubber stamps were made similar to those used on the stolen papers, signatures were copied, and a complete set of forged documents was prepared for the *Arthur* and her crew. On their arrival in Shetland they were smudged with dirt and oil and handled by Larsen and others to give the impression of age.

While all this was going on, the *Arthur* was being converted. On deck special cradles were constructed to carry the 2-ton chariots for the 24-hour journey across the North Sea, and the ship's derrick was strengthened to lift them in and out of the water. Then, as it was essential to hide the chariot crews and dressers during the dangerous run past the guard-boat and up the inner reaches of the fjord, a secret compartment was built between the engine-room and the hold to keep them out of sight, and two eyebolts were fitted to the *Arthur*'s keel for towing the chariots deep underwater. The hold itself would contain a cargo of peat, a commodity that was common to both Shetland and Norway.

Finally preparations had to be made for the crews of *Arthur* and the chariots to escape after the attack, as without Trondheim-stamped papers there could be no question of them attempting a return passage past the guard-boat. This part of the operation was in the hands of Herbert Hegelsen and Herluf Nygaard in Trondheim. After the attack the chariot crews would make their way to the south shore of the fjord where cars would be waiting to take them to the Swedish frontier. The *Arthur*'s crew and the two dressers would then scuttle *Arthur* and make their way to another part of the fjord where a lorry filled with hay in which they could hide would also be waiting. If either or both of these arrangements failed, there would be a rendezvous on top of a certain hill the following day; and if that failed, both crews would be equipped with maps and rations to find their own way to Sweden.

While these preparations were going on, *Tirpitz* was still at Bogen Bay, Narvik, but from agents' reports in

Trondheim it was learned that her berth there was in a full state of preparedness, and it was considered to be only a matter of time before she returned.

Now everything was ready for a full-scale exercise of the operation, as near to the real thing as could be devised. One evening the *Arthur*, with chariots and crews on board, sailed from Lunna Voe and set course south-west. She passed Cape Wrath on the north-eastern tip of Scotland, and entered the remote Loch Cairnbawn. At the far end of the loch, the hills behind her and protected by a row of nets, lay the old battleship *Rodney*; it was as similar a target to *Tirpitz* as they could get. They made fast alongside the depot-ship *Alecto*, and next day Admiral Sir Max Horton, who was staying on board *Rodney*, came over to meet them.

That evening the two dressers helped Brewster, Craig, Brown and Evans into their diving gear. The chariots were lowered and mounted, and the four men sped away towards the darkened battleship, their heads like four black balls skating along the surface of the water, then sliding silently beneath the waves. Then, and on subsequent evenings, they cut their way through the nets, laid dummy charges on the *Rodney*'s keel, and stole away unobserved. Was this how it would be on the night?

Now that everything that could be done had been done, they returned to Lunna Voe to await events. There, on 24 October, they heard that the dragon had returned to its lair.

Two days later, on a crisp, bright October morning, they set out at last on their great adventure. There were ten of them on board, Larsen and his three Norwegian crew — Björnöy in charge of the engine, Kalve and Strand — the four charioteers and the two dressers. Crown Prince Olaf of Norway and his Chief of Staff had flown up from London the day before to wish them well, and now, as they passed the depot-ship *Alecto* and exchanged blasts on their sirens, their 'god-father' Commander Fell gave them an encouraging farewell wave.

Not far from the coast a gale sprang up, and soon they were steaming into a rough easterly sea. Many were seasick, but they celebrated Brewster's twenty-fifth birthday with a tot of gin. Next day the weather abated, and in the evening they sighted mountains ahead. Next morning, very early, they nosed their way into the shelter of the islands, and Larsen dropped anchor in a small desolate bay.

Now it was time to lower the chariots into the water and fix them to the eyebolts in the hull for the 100-mile journey through the fjords. But no sooner had the tarpaulins and nets covering them been removed than there was a cry of 'Aircraft!' from the look-out in the bows. They had just about time to replace the coverings before the plane zoomed overhead.

This plane and others remained uncomfortably close all morning, so Larsen decided to move elsewhere. In another, even remoter anchorage, the chariots were lowered over the side, and Brewster and Evans, having changed into diving gear, soon had them positioned beneath the keel.

Then a rowing-boat was seen approaching, and the Britishers went below. The boat came up to the stern, and Larsen saw its occupant was a very old man with a beard. The old man started a desultory conversation, then noticed lying over the stern the rope that was holding the chariot. He pulled at it, and peered down. 'What's that for?' he said, pointing at the chariot. But Larsen had had enough. 'It's a special device for sweeping mines,' he said. 'We're working for the Germans, and if you tell anyone what you've seen we'll have the Gestapo after you. Here's a packet of butter. Now off with you.'

Since leaving Shetland the *Arthur* had been receiving regular radio messages, based on Spitfire reconnaissance flights, that *Tirpitz* was still at Trondheim. Now, with less than forty-eight hours to go before the attack (they were a day late on schedule but an extra day had been allowed for), and in waters where they might be searched at any time, they decided to throw the radio receiver overboard, together with the chariot's cradles, and any other gear not usually to be found in a local fishing-boat. The machine-gun they had been given for emergencies was stowed in the secret compartment along with the rucksacks and provisions for the escape.

Arthur's last stop was to be the village of Hestvik, on the east coast of an island only some fifteen miles from the Agdenes fortress. Here it had been arranged for Larsen to obtain from a local contact the latest information on German minefields and shipping control. But on the way, going up the Trondheimsleden, the engine began knocking badly. Björnöy thought it was the piston, and that water had got into the cylinder. It became worse and worse, and by the time they reached Hestvik at 11 p.m. the engine was about to die on them.

'You strip the engine,' said Larsen to Björnöy, 'while I go and see my contact.'

The contact's name was Nils Ström, a local storekeeper, and in his shop Larsen said, 'Do you need any peat?'

This was the cue for Ström to say, 'No, thank you. Did Odd Sörli send you?', but instead he said, 'Yes, we could do with all you've got.'

Christ, Larsen thought, have I come to the wrong man? He said, 'I can't let you have more than a little. Those were Odd Sörli's instructions.' For a moment Ström looked blank, then the truth dawned on him. He told Larsen about the control system in the fjord, and the papers the Germans most wanted to see. Then the two of them went back to the *Arthur* to see what had happened to the engine.

Björnöy, covered in oil, showed them the piston. 'Look,' he said, 'it's badly cracked. You can see. We can't sail with that.'

Ström took Björnöy to the house of the village blacksmith, and woke him up; he was a friend of Ström's and very reliable. For two hours Björnöy worked in his forge on the damaged piston, then as it was growing light he returned with it to the *Arthur*. After reassembling the engine and testing it, he said to Larsen, 'It should get us to Trondheim, but that's about all.'

It wasn't the happiest augury for the last part of their trip, but there was nothing to be done except hope. It was now 7 a.m.; Larsen and Björnöy had been up most of the night. 'We'll have a couple of hours' sleep,' said Larsen, 'and then we'll go. We must all be fresh for tonight.'

Bluffing their way past the guard-boat at Agdenes would, as everyone knew, be by far the most hazardous part of the voyage. When Larsen first sighted her below the Agdenes fortress, close to the northern shore, everyone went to their stations: Larsen and Björnöy in the wheelhouse, Strand at the engine, Kalve in the bows, the six Britishers in the secret compartment, with the electric switchboard in the engine-room covering the entrance to it.

So far that morning there had been a light breeze on the water, but as they neared the guard-boat Larsen observed to his horror that the sea was a flat calm. Looking over the side he could see the chariots clearly in the water. How could the Germans in the guard-boat fail to observe them too?

A hundred feet from the guard-boat Larsen gave the order to stop engines, and the familiar tonk-tonk of the motor abruptly ceased. A group of German sailors in the bows watched the *Arthur* approach, and as she eased alongside Larsen saw one of them staring at the water around the stern. Had he seen the chariots? Kalve, in the *Arthur*'s bows, threw a heaving line across to the German boat, and by lucky chance it landed on the sailor's shoulders. His attention distracted, he hauled in the line to secure the *Arthur* alongside. The captain of the guard-boat, a lieutenant, stepped on board.

'Papers!' he said.

Larsen gave him the forged documents, hoping that a glance would be sufficient, and they would soon be on their way. But the lieutenant went down the hatch to the cabin, sat down at the mess-table, and spread the papers before him.

'I see you come from Kristiansund,' he said, 'do you know my friend the harbourmaster, Lieutenant Ormann?'

Larsen wondered if this was a trap.

'Yes,' he said vaguely.

'He is an old friend of mine,' said the lieutenant, 'we went to school together.'

The lieutenant continued his leisurely scrutiny of the papers so long that in the darkness of the secret compartment the Britishers wondered if there had been a hitch. If so, they had the machine-gun and revolvers with them, and were prepared to fight.

'What is your cargo?' asked the lieutenant.

'*Torö*,' said Larsen (the Norwegian for peat).

'What is that?'

Larsen resisted an impulse to use the English word.

'Stuff for burning,' said Larsen, 'you dig it from the ground.'

'How do you spell it?' Larsen told him, and he carefully wrote it down.

'Any radio on board?'

'No.'

'Cameras?'

'No.'

'Passengers?'

Larsen thought of the six men below.

'No.'

The lieutenant said, *'Hier ist Ihr Ausweis'* and handed him the permit. 'You will give this to the harbourmaster at Trondheim on arrival.'

They went on deck. The lieutenant peered into the

wheelhouse, and down into the engine-room, then with a wave indicated to Larsen that he could go.

The lines were cast off, Larsen put the engine slow ahead. The water frothed at the stern, hiding the chariots from view. Slowly the guard-boat dropped astern.

In the *Arthur* the relief was tremendous. The chariot crews and dressers were released from their compartment and came on deck. Everyone wanted to shout and sing. Now there was nothing but forty miles of clear water between them and their target, between the little St George and the huge dragon, lying unsuspecting in its lair at the head of the fjord.

All afternoon the *Arthur* chugged slowly along the northern side of the fjord. The sea remained calm and the weather fine. There was a lot of shipping going in either direction. When a destroyer, outward bound, passed them, they had to slow right down to prevent its wash rocking the chariots.

At dusk they reached the end of the south-eastern leg of the fjord, and turned north. Here there was a slight change in the weather; a wind had risen and clouds were gathered ahead. The dimmed lights of Trondheim came abeam, and they could see against the night sky the twin spires of its cathedral. There were fifteen miles to go.

'Better get ready,' said Larsen.

Craig and Evans went below, and the dressers helped them into their diving suits. Brewster and Brown followed. The moment for which they had all been waiting was now at hand; the long months of training, the perilous and successful journey through the fjords — all were now about to come to fruition. They were about to try to sink the *Tirpitz*; somehow the idea seemed too fantastic to be true. Brewster was putting on the lower half of his diving dress when there was a sudden jolt, and he was thrown sideways.

'The weather's worsening,' somebody said.

For Larsen in the wheelhouse, it was worsening more

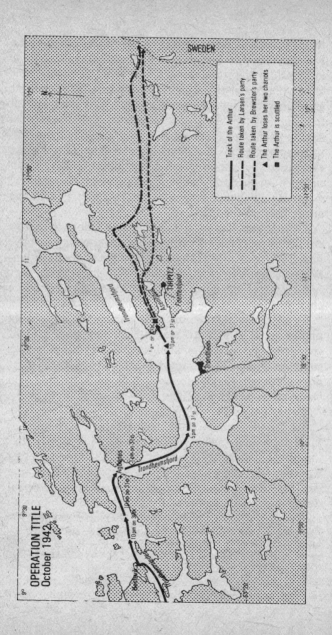

OPERATION TITLE
October 1942

SWEDEN

Trondheimsfjord

Trondheimsfjord

TIRPITZ
Feelfjord

Asenfjord

Trondheim

Herdla

Legend:
——— Track of the Arthur
– – – Route taken by Larsen's party
–··– Route taken by Brewster's party
▲ The Arthur loses her two chariots
■ The Arthur is scuttled

10pm on 30th
11pm on 30th
5pm or 31st
10pm or 31st
1am or 1st

than he dared believe. In the last half hour the wind had freshened considerably. The ship was steaming into a nasty head sea, at one moment her bows riding the crest of the waves, at the next plunging into the trough. With every rise and fall of the ship there would be a similar rise and fall for the chariots. How long could the towing wires stand the strain?

There was a loud thud, heard by everyone, as one of the chariots rising sharply upwards, hit the propeller. Then, suddenly, the *Arthur*'s motion eased.

'I think the chariots have gone,' said Larsen. 'We'll have to inspect them and see.'

They made their way towards the shore, and in a sheltered bay Evans in his diving suit went over the side. He surfaced a moment later with the news that everyone had feared: both chariots were gone.

In the little wheelhouse British and Norwegians looked at each other in anguish and dismay. To have come as far as this, to have brought themselves and their weapons to within striking distance of their target, then at the eleventh hour to be robbed of it, was something that did not bear thinking about. Nobody said anything; there was nothing to say.

'Well, we proceeded up Trondheimsfjord, and the weather was really quite fine, but as dusk fell, it started to deteriorate, and as we turned the corner to the north-east, a small gale sprang up. This caused the Arthur *to bob up and down a bit, and the chariots started to bump on the bottom of the ship. This was a bit worrying, so I asked Larsen, could we stop, but we were near Trondheim at the time, and he said he didn't think it advisable. So we went on at slow speed to reach the* Tirpitz *and have the job done before daylight.*

'Shortly after this the bumping became worse, and all of a sudden there was an almighty clatter, and something hit the propeller. Larsen said, the chariots have gone, I can tell by the steering. Well, that was a desperate blow, but we still hoped that perhaps only one of the chariots had gone, and we made for a bit of sheltered water, and Able Seaman Evans went down, and told us there was nothing there at all.

87

There could be no question of going back down the fjord: their papers had not been stamped at Trondheim, and anyway the engine was on its last legs. All that was left to them was to scuttle the *Arthur* and make their way ashore. They were nowhere near where the Trondheim resistance people were waiting, so, with emergency provisions and maps, they would have to walk the sixty miles to Sweden on their own.

At two in the morning, having thrown the peat overboard, five of them went ashore in the dinghy. One returned to the *Arthur*, and when they had opened the seacocks and bored holes below the water-line, the rest went ashore too. The ten men set off together towards the east, and after reaching a wood they lay down to sleep. Then, because such a large party might arouse suspicion, they decided to split: Larsen, Kalve, Craig, Evans and Tebb in one party, Brewster, Brown, Causer, Björnöy and Strand in the other.

After a variety of adventures and some hardship in the snows and bitter cold, both parties reached the Swedish frontier. Brewster's party, keeping to the high ground, all crossed over safely, but Larsen's group, coming lower down because of exhaustion to Evans, was challenged by Norwegian frontier guards. There was an exchange of shots; one of the guards and Evans was hit. The rest of the group found their way across the border.

Next day the Germans found Evans in a deserted hut to which he had crawled, took him to hospital and nursed him back to health. Under interrogation by the Gestapo he told them everything he knew about the chariots and their functions; then, his usefulness over, and on Hitler's orders, he was shot.

A week later the rest of the party were flown to England. In Trondheim the *Arthur* was raised (her masts were showing above the water), and as a result of the information supplied by Evans her various secrets were uncovered.

And at the end of Foettenfjord, hardly aware of all the fuss that had so concerned her, the *Tirpitz* quietly went on with her refit.

6. A New Weapon: The X-craft

Tirpitz's refit lasted for three months, and despite the lack of docking facilities the workmen sent from Germany did wonders, including putting a caisson round the stern and unshipping the huge rudder.

Occupation for the men was again uppermost in the mind of Captain Topp. As only a skeleton crew was needed for duty during the refit, seasonal leave in Germany was granted for the ship's company in watches. For those that remained there was daily ski-ing, and in the evenings films and concert parties. So many rats were found on board that a reward of five marks or a bottle of schnaps was offered for every rat tail handed in. Recognising a good thing when they saw one, a group of stokers made artificial rats' tails out of old packing, and collected several bottles of schnaps before their ruse was discovered.

At Christmas, a big fir tree was set up on deck, the messes were decorated with paper streamers, and on 31 December everyone sat down to a special New Year's Eve dinner. Each member of the crew received a bottle of wine, an extra tobacco ration, a packet of sweets and a book. After dinner in the wardroom there was a mock trial, and Lieutenant Commander Weber, the gunnery officer, did an imitation of Hitler, to which no one objected.

At midnight the captain addressed the ship's company on the loudspeakers. He thanked them for their cheerfulness and good discipline. They had expected, when they first came to Norway, to be engaged in a series of actions in the Arctic and the North Atlantic, 'even as far as the coast of France'. But it was not to be. 'We grit our teeth and bow to the decision of our superiors, even though it is hard for us. We serve the German Navy, and we must obey orders.' He concluded with a message of hope. 'We enter this new year . . . in the sure knowledge that when the moment comes for us to be put to the highest test, we shall be ready for it. I wish you all a happy new year.'

Meanwhile, on that same New Year's evening, 500 miles to the north, other units of the German Navy were being put to the test in an action that was to have far-reaching effects for all of them. Vice-Admiral Kummetz had received orders to take his flagship *Hipper*, together with the *Lützow* and six destroyers, to operate against the latest Russian convoy, JW 51B. Once again the German Navy had been given the opportunity to achieve a resounding success against inferior forces; once again hesitancy and half-heartedness reaped their own reward. The British lost a destroyer and a minesweeper, the Germans lost a destroyer and the *Hipper* was badly damaged. The convoy sailed through unharmed.

Preliminary reports from Narvik had indicated to Raeder that a victory had been achieved, so when Hitler first heard the true story from a BBC broadcast he was beside himself with rage. He sent for Raeder in his head-quarters in East Prussia and harangued him for over an hour on the uselessness, now and previously, of the German heavy ships. They were fit only for the scrap heap, he said; their crews would be better employed in U-boats, their guns on coastal defence.

For Raeder this was the end. He had commanded the German Navy for fourteen years, and was now sixty-six. So long as Hitler had given him a more or less free hand, his work had been tolerable. But to be lectured by a man who did not possess the glimmerings of the meaning of sea power, and to see the work of a lifetime destroyed in an instant, was too much. On 30 January 1943 he resigned, and proposed either Admiral Carls at Kiel or the submarine commander, Admiral Dönitz, to take his place. Hitler chose Dönitz.

Hitler had expected Dönitz to submit to his views, but

after considering the proposal Dönitz rejected it. If the big ships were to be dismantled, they would have to return to Germany, with all the risks that entailed; in the breakers' yards they would tie up a labour force for months in non-productive work; transferring their guns to coastal defence would raise more problems than it solved; and finally there was the question of morale. Technically the German heavy ships were among the finest in the world. What would the Navy think of a policy that condemned them to the scrap heap?

So Dönitz told Hitler that while he would agree to dismantling some of the cruisers, such as the damaged *Hipper*, the *Leipzig* and the *Köln*, he believed there was still a role for *Tirpitz*, *Scharnhorst* and *Lützow*. Stationed in the far north, they could still pose a threat to the Russian convoys and so relieve pressure on the eastern front, as well as helping (a point he knew Hitler would accept) in the defence of Norway. Moreover, whenever an opportunity presented itself the ships should attack the enemy boldly. Reluctantly Hitler agreed.

By 4 January 1943 *Tirpitz* had finished her refit and began sea and gunnery trials in Trondheimsfjord. A month later Topp was promoted to rear-admiral and handed over command to Captain Hans Meyer, a tall, thin, quiet man, well versed in naval history, who had lost an arm fighting against the socialists in 1919. In his two years in command, Topp had seen the *Tirpitz*'s best days; they had been a time of hope and expectation, if not fulfilment. From now on, even hope and expectation were dimmed. On 11 March Magne Hassel watched the battleship leave Trondheim for the last time. '*Tirpitz*, two destroyers and two torpedo-boats passed Agdenes outward bound at 0850 11 March.' Next day she joined *Scharnhorst* and *Lützow* in Altenfjord.

A little earlier, in London, Winston Churchill wrote one of his celebrated memos. It was addressed to the Chief of Combined Operations, the First Sea Lord, the Chiefs of the Air Staff and Bomber Command, and the Paymaster General:

> Have you given up all plans of doing anything to *Tirpitz* . . .? We heard a lot of talk about it five months ago which all petered out.
> I should be much obliged if you would take stock of the position, if possible together, and thereafter give me a report. It is a terrible thing that this prize should be waiting, and no one able to think of a way of winning it.

In fact another weapon to destroy tne menace had been fully tried and exercised, and now only waited an opportunity to be tested in action.

During 1942 the building of the X-craft or midget submarines and the training of their crews went on apace. On 26 August the first of them, X-3, after successful trials in Portland harbour, was loaded on to a railway truck and taken to Faslane on the Clyde, from where she was towed downstream to a base at Port Bannatyne in the Kyle of Bute. Her captain designate was Lieutenant Donald Cameron, RNR, and his first lieutenant John Lorimer; an engine-room artificer completed the crew of three.

X-4 was the next to arrive, under the command of Lieutenant Godfrey Place, DSC (an amiable officer with a habit of losing his own clothing and borrowing other people's). X-5 reached Faslane on the day that Kummetz was making his abortive sortie against convoy JW 51B. X-6 arrived in January 1943, and the remaining four shortly after. All had been built with the object of attacking *Tirpitz* and other large enemy units. During early exercises there was a nasty moment when X-3, under Lorimer, sank, and he and two trainees only just managed to escape from the bottom. On another occasion a sub-lieutenant was washed overboard from the casing of X-4 and never seen again.

In the early summer the boats transferred to Loch

Cairnbawn, just as the chariots had done, and carried out intensive exercises, cutting their way through nets and laying dummy charges beneath the keels of the battleship *Howe*. Another sub-lieutenant was lost while net-cutting, so it was decided to add a qualified diver to each X-craft's crew. On off-duty days the crews visited the villages of Kylesku and Drumbeg for scones and fresh eggs, fought mock battles in the heather, and supported local *ceilidhs* with their own highly original interpretations of Highland dancing.

It had been originally planned to attack the *Tirpitz* in Trondheim, a journey that the X-craft could have made under their own power. But with *Tirpitz*'s move to Altenfjord they would have to be towed. How? Fishing-boats like the *Arthur* did not have the pulling power, and in any case were the wrong boats for that area. They could be carried on board their depot-ship and released off the coast, but a sighting by enemy aircraft could then jeopardise the whole operation. In the end it was decided they would make the 1000-mile journey in tow of parent submarines.

Next, as with the chariots, it was essential to have the latest intelligence on *Tirpitz*'s whereabouts. One source for this was a courageous Norwegian named Torstein Raaby; earlier in the war he had been operating a secret transmitter at Tromsö, but had had to flee to Sweden and thence to England. He was returned to Norway with a radio set in the Norwegian submarine *Ula*, made his way to Altenfjord, and managed to obtain a job as a roadman at Alta. Here he set up his radio and, using the receiving aerial of his neighbour, a German officer, as a transmitter, sent daily intelligence reports to London on the dispositions of the German fleet. He also made a detailed sketch map of the fleet anchorages and the nets guarding them and took them over the border to Sweden, where they found their way first to Captain Denham in Stockholm, thence to the Admiralty in London.

Air reconnaissance was harder to arrange, as Altenfjord was beyond the range of British bases. Approaches were made to the Russians, and after some initial reluctance they gave permission for half a dozen Spitfires to be temporarily based at Vaenga, within easy flying distance of Altenfjord.

By mid-August training was complete, and a date for attacking the German ships fixed for the period 20–25 September. This meant leaving Cairnbawn not later than 11 September. Because of the appallingly cramped living conditions in the X-craft (vertical clearance was no more than 4½ feet) it was decided that passage crews should man the boats for the eight days it would take to reach the release zone, with the operational crews resting in the parent submarines.

On 30 August the submarine depot-ship *Titania*, under Commander Fell, sailed into Cairnbawn in the company of the submarines *Thrasher*, *Turbulent*, *Seanymph*, *Sceptre*, *Syrtis* and *Stubborn*. For three days parents and midgets exercised in towing and transferring crews, and on 6 September the midgets were hoisted on board their depot-ship *Bonaventure* for the fitting of the 2-ton side-charges of amatex explosive. All that was left now was the briefing of the crews.

And then next day, 7 September, came disturbing news: a signal from Raaby, almost immediately confirmed by the first Spitfire to fly from Vaenga to Altenfjord. The German fleet anchorage was empty; the birds had flown.

If the crews of *Tirpitz* and *Scharnhorst* hoped that their transference to Altenfjord would at last bring them some action, they were in for further disappointment – for on the recommendation of Admiral Sir Bruce Fraser, Tovey's successor as C-in-C Home Fleet, the Cabinet had decided that their presence in Altenfjord made the sailing of further Arctic convoys too perilous to risk.

So all Dönitz's bold schemes of offensive action were set at nought; his ships, as one writer put it, were all dressed up with no place to go. In a way their presence had achieved their purpose — preventing supplies going through to Russia — and at no risk to themselves. But this was small comfort to their crews.

And so the spring and summer months of 1943 went by, and in *Tirpitz*, *Scharnhorst* and *Lützow* the men became more and more depressed. In Foettenfjord at least there had been a nearby town and other human beings; in this desolate anchorage there was nothing.

So it became imperative to find some minor operation for them to perform, and eventually one was found. The Russian and Norwegian settlements at Spitzbergen, 600 miles to the north, had been evacuated earlier in the war, but since then parties of men from both sides had used the island for meteorological intelligence. At present a British and Norwegian team were there, transmitting regular weather reports to London, and protected by a small Norwegian garrison.

The destruction of the wireless installations and capture of the meteorologists hardly merited the attention of a powerful naval force, let alone justified the expenditure of so much scarce fuel, but there was nothing else to hand. On 6 September *Tirpitz*, *Scharnhorst* and ten destroyers, under Admiral Kummetz, sailed from Altenfjord, and, flying the British Navy's White Ensign, arrived at Spitzbergen at dawn the next day. Here they bombarded the puny defences as well as the wireless and meteorological installations (the first and only time *Tirpitz* fired her main armament at a surface target), then landed a 600-strong commando force to blow up anything that remained and take prisoners. They were accompanied by a team of cameramen who took stirring action pictures for a public to whom defeats were now becoming more common than victories, and who were beginning to doubt whether the German surface fleet was still afloat. Sixty-three prisoners were taken; but three of the destroyers were damaged by shore batteries.

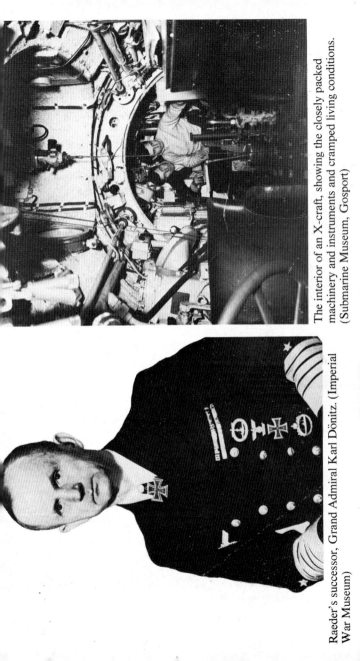

Raeder's successor, Grand Admiral Karl Dönitz. (Imperial War Museum)

The interior of an X-craft, showing the closely packed machinery and instruments and cramped living conditions. (Submarine Museum, Gosport)

One of the installations at Spitzbergen goes up in flames. (B.B.C. documentary programme *Target 'Tirpitz'*)

The commanding officers of five of the X-craft chosen to attack *Tirpitz:* Lieutenants Hudspeth, McFarlane, Martin, Place (second from right) and Cameron (right). (Submarine Museum, Gosport)

erial photograph of Altenfjord and Kaafjord, showing *Tirpitz* (arrowed) d the approximate route taken by X-5, X-6 and X-7. (Popperfoto)

.A.F. reconnaissance photograph of *Tirpitz* taken shortly after the -craft attack. Note the oil slicks from her damaged tanks. (David rown/Imperial War Museum)

The carriers *Victorious, Furious, Emperor, Pursuer* and *Searcher*
approach the flying-off position off the Norwegian coast. (Imperial War
Museum)

Preparation for the Fleet Air Arm attack on *Tirpitz*, 3 April 1944.
Briefing of aircrews by the Commander, Flying. (Imperial War Museum)

he target. The unsuspecting *Tirpitz* at anchor behind her nets in
aafjord. (Popper foto)

30 a.m., 3 April 1944. *Tirpitz* has weighed anchor and is about to
oceed to sea. Smoke has just been released from the canisters ashore,
ıt too late to conceal her. (Robert Hunt Library)

Dr Barnes Wallis. Before the war he designed the airships R-100 and R-101, and later the Wellington bomber. (Keystone)

Wing-Commander J. B. Tait who led all three Lancaster attacks against the *Tirpitz*. (Keystone)

The weapon that eventually was to bring *Tirpitz*'s life to an end. Dr. Barnes Wallis's six-ton Tallboy bomb. (Imperial War Museum)

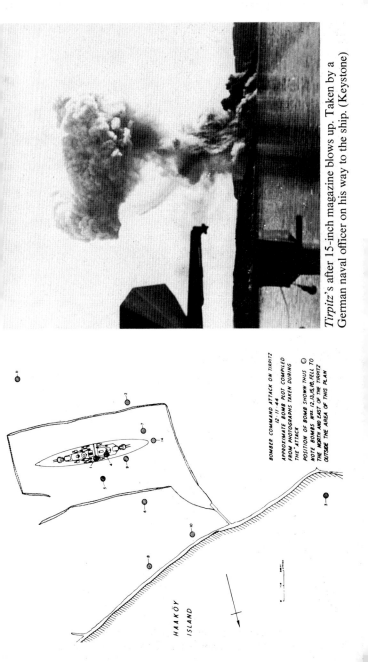

BOMBER COMMAND ATTACK ON TIRPITZ
12·11·44
APPROXIMATE BOMB PLOT COMPILED
FROM PHOTOGRAPHS TAKEN DURING
THE ATTACK
POSITION OF BOMB SHOWN THUS ○
NOTE BOMBS Nos. 12,13,15,16, FELL TO
THE NORTH AND EAST OF THE TIRPITZ
OUTSIDE THE AREA OF THIS PLAN

HAAKÖY
ISLAND

Tirpitz's after 15-inch magazine blows up. Taken by a
German naval officer on his way to the ship. (Keystone)

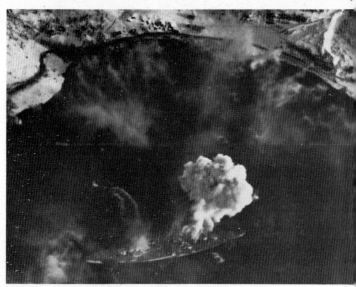

Tirpitz in trouble. Smoke from the canisters ashore mingles with that of explosions on board as the bombs register direct hits (Captain Eveleigh)

Germans walking on the upturned keel of *Tirpitz*. Altogether some eighty seven men were rescued through holes cut into the hull. (B.B.C. documentary programme *Target 'Tirpitz'*)

One of the British meteorologists at Spitzbergen was a Mr E. C. Dabner, who, when the bombardment started, took refuge in a disued mine-shaft. Wounded when one of the landing party threw a hand-grenade into the shaft, he was soon captured. 'I went in a boat along the fjord, and as we came alongside a big ship, I thought, Good Heavens, the *Tirpitz*. I never expected to see her, let alone go aboard her. I was taken to the sickbay where they treated me very well. I was the only Englishman aboard, and felt it an honour to be referred to as "the Englishman".'

Next day the force was back in Altenfjord. Here an unseemly discord broke out between the men of *Tirpitz* and *Scharnhorst*. To boost morale further, there was a large-scale issue of Iron Crosses Second Class for those who had taken part in the operation. The crew of *Tirpitz*, having seen no action for eighteen months, were quite happy to receive them; but the men of *Scharnhorst*, having won their medals the hard way, in the North Sea, the Atlantic and the Channel, thought the award of Iron Crosses ridiculous for so piffling an operation, and said so forcibly.

Next day another Spitfire flew over Altenfjord and sent an encouraging signal to Loch Cairnbawn: the birds were back in their nest.

7. Operation Source

At 4 p.m. on 11 September, the six parent submarines, with their brood in tow, left Cairnbawn at two-hourly intervals and headed north. In daylight hours both parents and midgets would remain submerged, the midgets surfacing for fifteen minutes every six hours to ventilate the boat; at night the parents would travel on the surface to recharge their batteries. Communication would be by telephone wires threaded through the towing ropes.

The first three days of the passage, with each pair of submarines spread twenty miles apart, were uneventful. On the 14th, as a result of further Spitfire reconnaissance, they received a signal giving up-to-date news of the enemy ships. *Tirpitz* was anchored off a spit of land at the end of Kaafjord, a finger of Altenfjord; *Scharnhorst* was at the head of Kaafjord, near the entrance; *Lützow* was in Lange Fjord, ten miles to the north. All were surrounded by nets. In addition there was a double row of nets stretching across the entrance to Kaafjord. The targets were to be: *Tirpitz*, X-5, X-6 and X-7; *Lützow*, X-8; and *Scharnhorst*, X-9 and X-10. The attacks were to be made between 1 a.m. and 8 a.m. on 22 September.

The next three days were less happy. In the early hours of the 15th the tow between *Seanymph* and X-8 parted. X-8 surfaced, was unable to find *Seanymph*, but by chance came across *Stubborn* and X-7. She lost them soon after by steering the wrong course, and it wasn't until the evening of the 16th that *Seanymph* at last found her. After thirty-six hours on their own, the passage crew were exhausted, and the operational crew were transferred by rubber dinghy to relieve them.

Meanwhile a greater misfortune had occurred to X-9. In the early morning of the 16th, she dived after fifteen minutes on the surface. Six hours later her parent *Syrtis* dropped hand-grenades for her to surface, but she did not appear. It was found the tow had parted. *Syrtis* retraced her steps along the line of advance but there was no sign of X-9. She continued searching all day and most of the night, but X-9 was never seen again. Probably, when the tow rope parted, the boat had taken a downward dive and been crushed by the pressure before the crew had time to correct it. Now there were only five boats to make the attack.

On the morning of the 17th misfortune struck again. The wayward X-8, once more in tow of *Seanymph*, was having increasing difficulties with her trim. Air could be heard escaping from the buoyancy chamber in the starboard side-charge, and with the boat listing further and further to starboard there was no alternative but to jettison the charge. This inevitably meant a list to port, and when it was reported that the port side-charge was flooding the captain had to jettison this too. With all her explosives gone X-8 was now out of the operation; she was therefore scuttled and her passage crew transferred to *Seanymph*. Now there were four.

Between the 17th and the 19th *Truculent, Thrasher, Sceptre* and *Syrtis* made their landfalls on the Norwegian coast. On the 19th, a Sunday, Lieutenant Alexander, captain of *Truculent*, held divine service for those not on duty, forty feet below the surface. He read the familiar, traditional prayer for those at sea: 'Oh, Eternal Lord God, who alone spreadest out the heavens and ruleth the raging of the sea . . .', and there was a special prayer 'for our comrades in arms about to embark on their hazardous operation'.

By dawn on the 20th all four operational and passage crews had been safely exchanged. Even so events were not without incident. On the evening of the 19th and again on the 20th Lieutenant Jupp in *Syrtis* sighted a U-boat on the surface. Both were sitting targets, but his orders were not to make any enemy attacks for fear of jeopardising the operation, and he let them go by.

A more unpleasant incident happened to Godfrey Place in X-7. A floating mine had become entangled in the tow rope to *Stubborn*; it drifted down it and became wedged on X-7's bow. With great presence of mind Place made his way along the casing, and spent seven minutes trying to push it clear with his foot – 'the first time in my life', he said afterwards, 'that I ever shoved a mine clear by its horns.'

Between 6.30 p.m. and 8 p.m. on the 20th Lieutenant Henty-Creer in X-5, Lieutenant Cameron in X-6, Lieutenant Place in X-7, and Lieutenant Hudspeth in X-10 (whose target, since the mishaps to X-8 and X-9, had been shifted from *Scharnhorst* to *Tirpitz*) slipped the tow ropes from their parent submarines and pointed their small craft east, towards the German minefields that guarded the approaches to Altenfjord. They were all unaware of each other's whereabouts, but in twenty-four hours' time they were scheduled to reach Tommelholm, one of a group of small islands near the entrance to Kaafjord, just four miles from the *Tirpitz*. At dawn the day after they would attack.

Under a bright moon and with the northern lights shimmering in the sky, all four X-craft crossed the minefield safely and entered the inner leads.

X-10 dived at dawn on the 21st, intending to travel submerged all day up Söröy Sound and Stjern Sound. But first the motor of the periscope failed, so it was impossible to hoist it, then the gyro compass went off the board. So Lieutenant Hudspeth bottomed in a small fjord north of Sternöy to make repairs. The crew worked all day, but it soon became evident that water had seeped into the electrical equipment, and little could be done. Underwater the boat was almost blind.

At dusk Hudspeth surfaced, and steering by magnetic compass set course up Stjern Sound, keeping to the north shore. By midnight he was into Altenfjord, and hoping to be at the entrance to Kaafjord by dawn. A vessel appeared ahead and X-10 dived. When Hudspeth tried to raise the periscope, there was a crackling noise and a smell of burnt rubber: the motor, partially repaired, had burnt out again. The gyro compass was still out of action, and now the light in the magnetic compass failed.

So Hudspeth again surfaced, and steered for Tommelholm, two miles from the Kaafjord entrance. There he took X-10 to the bottom, and once more set about repairs. It was now 2 a.m. on the 22nd, the morning of the attack. They had just six hours in which to make good the damage, find a way through the Kaafjord nets, and lay their mines under *Tirpitz*. On the face of it, the chances seemed slim.

X-6's troubles were of a different nature. She had developed a list of 10 degrees to starboard during the passage, due to flooding of the starboard side-charge, and this now increased to 15 degrees. Cameron tried to correct it by ditching excess stores and shifting others to port. In addition the periscope was leaking and badly misted over.

After crossing Söröy Sound X-6 dived at 1.25 a.m. on the 21st, when it was growing light, and for the rest of the day continued submerged up Stjern Sound and Altenfjord. At dusk she was near Tommelholm and surfaced close inshore to charge her batteries. Cameron climbed on to the casing and saw the floodlights on the Kaafjord nets two miles away; there was no sign of any other X-craft. He observed the headlights of a car going along the coast road, and wrote in his log: 'Wondered if it might be carrying the German admiral, and speculated on his reactions tomorrow if all went well.'

There were one or two scares during the night, such as the door of a hut close to the water opening and spilling out men, whose voices could clearly be heard. Later a German torpedo-boat appeared from nowhere and there was an emergency dive. Just before 1.45 a.m. on the

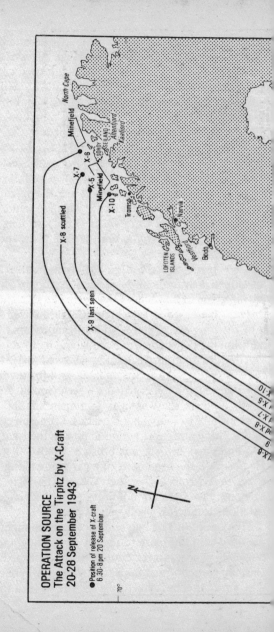

OPERATION SOURCE
The Attack on the Tirpitz by X-Craft
20-28 September 1943

● Position of release of X-craft
6.30-8 pm 20 September

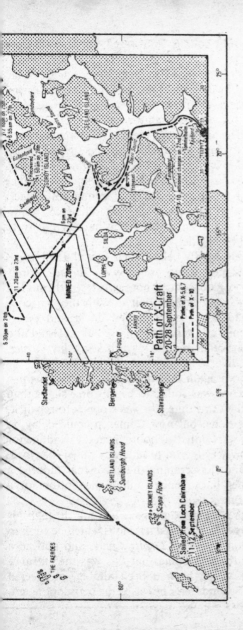

Path of X-Craft
20-28 September

Paths of X 5,6 & 7 ———
Path of X 10 – – – –

THE FAEROES

SHETLAND ISLANDS
Sumburgh Head

ORKNEY ISLANDS
Scapa Flow

Sailed from Loch Cairnbaw
11-12 September

60°

0°

5°E

Sladlandet

Bergen

Stavanger

FUGLOY

ARVOY

LOPPA

SILDA

MINED ZONE

6 pm on
23rd

11.20pm on 23rd

5.30pm on 24th

Sandholm

Gulnarfjord

Helicovered

1.50am on 26th

SORØY ISLAND

Salin Sound

Sandsfjord

6.55am on 27th

7.45pm on 25th

SELAND ISLAND

Brennsund

Stjernsund

position

Fustvik

X-10 abandoned charges on 22nd

Tommelholm

Kaafjord

TIRPITZ

25°

20°

10°

22nd Cameron set course, submerged, for the Kaafjord nets.

But he hadn't gone far when the periscope again began clouding over. Twice Cameron stopped to repair it, but with little success. Without an effective periscope, how would he find his way through the nets?

By 4.45 a.m. he had reached the nets, and was considering how best to negotiate them when he sighted first a ferryboat coming up Kaafjord outward bound and then a coaster about to pass into the fjord. Knowing the entrance gate would be open only for a few minutes longer, knowing too that his craft was too blind to follow submerged, he made an instant decision: 'Stand by to surface. Stand by engine.'

His crew could hardly believe their ears. To sail into a heavily guarded enemy anchorage *on the surface*. Surely the men on the gate control-boat *must* see them. But Cameron knew what he was doing. With the periscope housed and the boat well trimmed down and partly hidden in the coaster's wake, X-6 passed unmolested into Kaafjord. At the other end, 4000 yards away, lay *Tirpitz*.

'Dive, dive, dive!'

They slid down again into the black, friendly depths. Here the periscope was found to be in worse shape than ever, and for the third time X-6 was stopped to repair it. Little could be done, but now Cameron could delay no longer, as they were only two hours from the deadline for the attack. Slowly Cameron felt his way down the fjord, once in his blindness scraping the cable that moored a destroyer to her buoy, once fouling the bottom of a floating pontoon.

A little before 7 a.m. Cameron, looking through his fogged periscope, saw some dark blobs which he took to be the floatation buoys of *Tirpitz*'s nets, and noticed a space between them. Hoping that this was the entrance for boats, for which he had been aiming, he steered straight for it. Seconds later he raised the periscope again.

The blobs had disappeared; only a great, grey, indistinct mass showed through the fogged lens. It was the *Tirpitz*, 100 yards away. They were through.

Godfrey Place in X-7 had the most trouble-free early passage of the lot. On passage through the Söröy mine-field on the evening of the 20th he sighted Henty-Creer and X-5 (whom he had last seen in Loch Cairnbawn ten days before) and they exchanged greetings of 'Good hunting' and 'Good luck'. He made the passage up Stjern Sound and Altenfjord without incident, and at 4.30 p.m. sighted the *Scharnhorst* steaming north (she was en route to gunnery exercises).

At dusk Place arrived at Tommelholm. He spent the night charging batteries and diving to avoid numerous small craft, but without sighting any of the others. He let the crew come on deck in turns for fresh air. 'It was a calm, peaceful evening,' he wrote later, 'we could hear the broadcasts from the tankers and supply ships down in the anchorage. It was hard to believe our target was only four miles away.'

Just before 1 a.m., a little earlier than Cameron, he set off for the Kaafjord nets. Like Cameron he was lucky in finding the gate open to let in a minesweeper, and was able to follow her through submerged. So far his journey had been according to the book. Now his difficulties began.

First he ran X-7 straight into nets reserved for *Lützow*, now empty. He took an hour to free himself, then, threading his way between the shipping at anchor, proceeded towards *Tirpitz*'s nets at seventy feet – it was unlikely, he thought, that they stretched that deep. But he was wrong; he went straight into them.

'Full astern. Empty the tanks.'

X-7 came up a few feet but only succeeded in pulling the meshes after her. Place thought how the buoys holding the nets on the surface must be jigging up and down, and that it could be only a matter of time before a look-out in *Tirpitz* spotted them. He went slow ahead, full astern, hard a starboard, hard a port, all to no avail. Just when he was thinking he might have to send his diver up to cut the meshes, the boat unexpectedly broke free.

'Ninety-five feet!'

Surely the nets would not stretch as deep as this; sixty feet was as low as British nets went.

'Slow ahead.'

But once again the boat came to a stop, and everyone could hear and feel the meshes scraping on the bow. Place could not understand it: the depth of water was only 120 feet; surely the nets did not stretch to the bottom. What he was not to know was that there were two sets of nets surrounding the *Tirpitz*; one that stretched downwards from the surface, and another, nearer the ship, that went upwards from the bottom. Without knowing it, he had passed under the net that stretched from the surface, and was now enmeshed in the one laid on the bottom.

Gently he eased X-7 out, and rose to the surface to see where he was.

'Up periscope!'

He grasped the periscope handles and put his head to the eyepiece. A hundred yards away, across clear water, rode the *Tirpitz*.

'Half ahead. Sixty feet.'

X-7 moved inexorably towards her target. Now nothing could stop her from accomplishing the great mission on which she had set out, for which her crew had been preparing for more than two years; time and place had coincided.

At thirty feet there was a slight bump as X-7's bows grazed the battleship's side.

'Stop.'

X-7 dropped below the huge hull, the shadow of the ship clearly visible through the glass scuttles. The time fuses on the explosives had already been set to one hour.

'Release port side-charge.'

The boat lifted slightly as the charge fell away to the bottom.

'Slow ahead.'

With marvellous calm Place manoeuvred his craft down the length of the ship until he reckoned he was beneath the after turrets.

'Release starboard side-charge.'

Once again the boat rose a little with the added buoyancy. The four members of the crew felt a sense of tremendous exhilaration. They had done what they had been asked to do; whatever happened now, nothing could ever take that away from them.

'Starboard twenty. Half ahead.'

Carefully Place pointed the bows of X-7 towards the nets. They had found a way through them with difficulty. Could they now find a way out?

'I thought the best thing was to come up to periscope depth and have a look and see where I was. We did just that, and miracle of miracles we were inside all the nets and there was no other obstacle between us and Tirpitz. So then it was half ahead, group up, 60 feet, and just as we were going down we touched the Tirpitz a glancing blow at about 30 feet. We slid gently underneath and through the glass scuttles I could see the full shadow of the ship above us. Bill stopped the boat, I set the time fuses to one hour, and we released one of the charges under what I took to be A and B turrets. After that it was a gentle cruise for 300 feet along the hull to where I estimated X and Y turrets to be, and there we dropped the other side charge.

'Then it was back out the way we came in, but I ran straight into the nets again. I tried every depth and angle, I must have crossed underneath the Tirpitz three or four times, but I still couldn't get out. By now time was ticking by, our charges were due to explode, and we were still only about 100 yards away. So I went fairly fast ahead, and with a tremendous blow in No 1 ballast tank we broke surface at a 60° angle, so the boat fell on top of the nets as she came out of the water and literally slid over to the other side . . . Shortly after this the charges did explode with a long roar.'

Extract from Rear-Admiral Godfrey Place's interview on the BBC documentary programme 'Target Tirpitz'.

*

On board the *Tirpitz* the day had started with the calling of the hands at 5 a.m. (7 a.m. German time). At the same time (and fortunately for Cameron and Place) the hydrophone listening watch was secured for routine maintenance. At 7 a.m. (9 a.m. German time) Captain Meyer sat down to breakfast in his cabin.

Seven minutes later, Cameron in X-6, working his way blindly along the western shore of the fjord, hit a rock and, with the boat momentarily out of control, surfaced. Before disappearing she was observed briefly by a petty officer in *Tirpitz*, but thought to be a porpoise. Five minutes later she surfaced again, off *Tirpitz*'s port beam. This time there was no doubt about it. A burst of small arms fire was directed at her (she was too near for the heavier armament to bear), the officer of the watch made the signal for close watertight doors, and Captain Meyer hurried to the bridge.

Seeing roughly his position through the blurred periscope, Cameron ordered full astern, and the half-alerted crew of *Tirpitz* (the bridge *should* have made the signal for action stations) watched fascinated as X-6 moved inevitably towards them. Sub-Lieutenant Leine went away in the ship's motor-boat, armed with hand-grenades and a grappling-hook, and reached X-6 as she bumped into the ship abreast of B turret.

Cameron, hearing the bump, ordered: 'Release side-charges.'

The four tons of amatex slid to join those of X-7 at the bottom under *Tirpitz*'s bow. The boat, lightened, came further out of the water.

'Open all main vents and No 2 Kingston. Slow astern.'

In a few minutes the boat would sink beneath them. Cameron opened the hatch, and with raised hands he and his crew came up on the casing and stepped into the launch. Leine had already secured his grappling rope to X-6, but with the boat going astern and sinking he had to cut it free to avoid the launch being pulled under. Leine

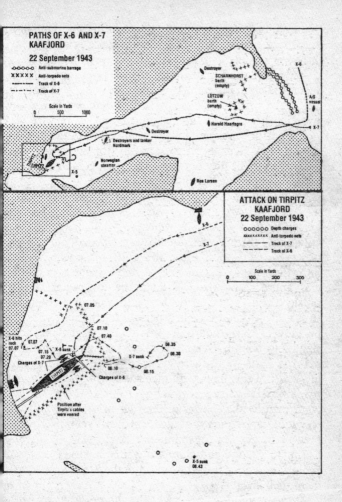

PATHS OF X-6 AND X-7
KAAFJORD

22 September 1943

○○○○○ Anti-submarine barrage
✕✕✕✕✕ Anti-torpedo nets
—·—·— Track of X-6
– – – – Track of X-7

Scale in Yards
0   500   1000

Destroyer

SCHARNHORST berth (empty)

X-6

LÜTZOW berth (empty)

A/S vessel

Destroyer

Harald Haarfagre

X-7

Destroyers and tanker Nordmark

Norwegian steamer

X-5

Ros Larsen

ATTACK ON TIRPITZ
KAAFJORD
22 September 1943

○○○○○○ Depth charges
✕✕✕✕✕✕ Anti-torpedo nets
– – – – Track of X-7
—·—·— Track of X-6

Scale in Yards
0   100   200   300

X-6

X-7

07.05

07.10

07.40

06.35

06.38

X-7 sunk

X-6 hits rock
07.07   07.07

07.15
07.20   X-6 sunk

06.10

06.15

Charges of X-7

TIRPITZ

Charges of X-6

Position after Tirpitz's cables were veered

X-5 sunk
06.43

went alongside the gangway, the crew of X-6 climbed to the quarter-deck, saluted, and were made prisoner.

Meyer's immediate concern was to move his ship as far out of harm's way as possible, so orders were given for the instant raising of steam. It would take at least an hour to get under way, so divers were piped to go down and examine the hull for limpet mines, and a big wire was prepared for scraping along the ship's bottom. The duty Arado crew were piped to stand by for launching, and destroyers in the fleet anchorage were ordered to carry out an anti-submarine patrol.

Only four minutes later a second submarine was seen to surface 100 yards away. This was X-7 trying to free herself from the nets in which she had again become entangled. Fire was immediately opened, hits were observed, and soon after the craft disappeared. Not knowing whether the midgets carried torpedoes or mines, and appreciating that he might be in greater danger outside the nets than inside, Meyer now decided not to put to sea, and instead gave instructions for the ship's bow to be moved to starboard (both submarines having been sighted to port) by veering and shortening the cables.

From all accounts there seems to have been some panic in *Tirpitz* at this time, with men running aimlessly to and fro, aware that disaster was about to strike them – a view confirmed by the actions of the four prisoners who were seen looking frequently at their watches – yet powerless to prevent it. Slowly the minutes ticked by as Cameron, Lorimer, Kendall and Goddard waited anxiously for the explosion they all hoped would sink the *Tirpitz*, yet spare them their own lives.

At twelve minutes past eight the charges went off with tremendous force, creating a whip effect that lifted the ship upwards and was felt from stem to stern. 'There was the most God Almighty bang,' said Lorimer. 'All the lights went out and I was thrown off my chair.' Kendall said, 'There was complete darkness. Fire sprinklers showered foam on us. The ship started to list to port. Seamen ran in all directions. Bursts of machine-gun fire were interspersed with the loud crashes of the secondary armament firing wildly. It was impossible to take it all in.' And one of the German sailors, Schimanski, said, 'Everybody was running around, nobody really knew what had happened to us.'

Because of the move of the ship's bows to starboard, the three charges originally placed under the forward keel plates had exploded some sixty yards away and were not as lethal as had been hoped; to the intense disappointment of the prisoners the *Tirpitz* remained afloat. Yet she had been severely, even critically, damaged. Many of the decks and passageways were buckled and twisted; A and C 15-inch turrets had been lifted off their turntables; many tons of water had entered the bottom compartments, one generator room and the after steering compartment being flooded. Range-finders, fire-control instruments, radio and radar equipment were all put out of action, and two Arado aircraft were severely damaged. As a result of Place's second charge placed aft, none of the three propeller shafts could be turned, and the port rudder was smashed. One man had been killed and fifty wounded, several with broken legs.

'We were taken on board Tirpitz's *quarter-deck and told to empty all our pockets, which we did. Then we were taken below, and put in a corridor, and I heard a lot of clanging of chains and whatnot, and I thought, oh dear, they're going to move the ship before our charges go off. Eventually the charges did go off, which shook us a bit; all the lights went off, and a foam extinguisher started to pour forth on my German guard who didn't like it very much. He grabbed me by the neck, and we went up on deck, and I was very disturbed the ship didn't appear to be sinking.*

'They lined us up before a group of guards with tommy guns; they were all very hostile and murmured Schweinhund *and other things. Then an interpreter came along and asked us how many boats were there and so on, but we just gave them our names*

111

and numbers. He got very annoyed and said that if we didn't play, he'd have to shoot us. He pointed at Lorimer and said to me, if you don't give the information, I shall have to shoot your comrade too. Oh, well, I said, you go ahead and shoot him.'

Extract from Edmund Goddard's interview on the BBC documentary programme 'Target Tirpitz'.

Half an hour later a third submarine was sighted off the starboard bow, some 250 yards beyond the nets. This was Henty-Creer's X-5, which had not been sighted since he and Place had exchanged greetings on their way in. She was hit repeatedly before disappearing, and then the destroyer Z-27 dropped depth-charges over the area where she had submerged. No trace of her or her crew was ever found.

The prisoners were taken below to be interrogated by the staff officer, Commander Emden. But it soon became clear that they were prepared to give no information beyond their names, ranks and numbers. Captain Meyer therefore, being a humane man and admiring the gallantry of their attack, ordered that they should be given coffee and schnaps and somewhere to sleep. Soon after, the door opened, and in came a dripping Godfrey Place, wearing a sweater, boots and long underpants.

After several fruitless attempts to find a way through the nets he had finally cleared them by surfacing at speed and at an angle and sliding over them. Then he had run into another net. The explosion of the charges had freed him from this, but had caused extensive damage to X-7. Her compass and diving gauges were out of action, so she could stay either on the surface or on the bottom, but lacked all manoeuvrability underwater. Place decided to escape on the surface, but as soon as he reached it he was met by a fusillade of fire which holed the boat in several places and destroyed his periscope.

There was nothing left but to abandon ship. The craft

surfaced again near a gunnery-target raft and Place opened the hatch and waved his white sweater in surrender. The others were about to follow when the boat, already awash, sank beneath him. Place swam to the raft and was picked up by a boat from *Tirpitz*.

Later that morning, a sixth survivor joined the others: Bob Aitken, another of Place's crew. His was a nightmare story. As the boat began to sink under the rush of water into the forward compartment, he, Bill Whittam and Willie Whitley descended slowly the 120 feet to the bottom. Their only chance of survival now was by Davis Escape Apparatus. This meant putting on water-tight oxygen masks, then flooding the craft slowly so that when the water reached their necks and the pressure outside was almost equal to that inside they could open the hatches and rise to the surface. It was agreed that Whittam should go up by the forward hatch, Whitley aft, and Aitken by whichever of the two was clear first.

Three of the vents letting in the water were blocked, so it rose very slowly. It took half an hour to reach their thighs and the cold was intense. When the water met the electrical circuits, the fuses exploded, the lights went out and the boat was filled with smoke and chlorine gas from the batteries. Crouching in the icy cold and darkness on the bottom of the sea, and breathing carefully through their masks, they waited for the water to reach their necks. It was another half-hour before it was level with their chests, and all the time the precious oxygen was giving out.

Now Aitken groped his way forward to see if he could help Whittam open the forward hatch. He couldn't see Whittam because of the dark, and he couldn't call to him because of his mask. He felt for him with his hands but there was nothing where Whittam should have been. Then his foot touched Whittam's body underwater. His oxygen had run out. Whittam was dead.

Aitken felt his way back aft. His own oxygen had almost

given out. He switched on the two small emergency bottles, but he knew they would give him only a few breaths apiece. In the after compartment he groped for Whitley, but found that Whitley was dead too. With the last of his oxygen almost gone, and feeling he was about to faint, he raised his hand to the hatch with a last despairing effort. It opened. He sped upwards to the surface, yet managed to remember to spread his escape apron in front of him to slow his speed and so avoid getting the bends. On the surface he drew great gulps of air into his starved lungs. A boat picked him up.

Next day Captain Meyer, anxious that his prisoners should not share the same fate as Able Seaman Evans of the chariots, had his prisoners transferred to Tromsö hospital and thereafter to Germany for internment as prisoners of war. There, a year later, Place and Cameron learned they had been awarded the Victoria Cross.

The remaining midget, X-10, had been unable to repair her defects off Tommelholm in time to take part in the attack. Hudspeth heard the charges go off, then regretfully decided he must jettison his own charges and rendezvous with the waiting parent submarines. It took him two days to reach the assembly area beyond the mine-fields. For the next four days he searched there without success, he and his crew becoming more and more depressed and weary in their cramped living space. On the evening of 27 December Hudspeth approached the final rendezvous position, a small bay in one of the outer islands, determined that if no contact was made he would have to try and take his boat around the North Cape to Murmansk. But just after midnight on the 28th his infra-red light was seen by *Stubborn*, and he and his exhausted crew were rescued.

So ended Operation SOURCE, which by any standards had been a huge success, imaginatively planned and brilliantly executed. The British knew almost immediately that the attack had succeeded. Ultra signals were intercepted from the destroyer *Erich Steinbrinck* reporting a heavy explosion at 8.12 a.m. (German time 10.12 a.m.) 60 metres to port of *Tirpitz* and letting in 500 cubic metres of water, and from the *Tirpitz* at 8.48 a.m. (G.T. 10.48 a.m.) requesting a ship capable of electric welding to be sent forthwith. The day after the attack a Spitfire reported that while *Scharnhorst* and *Lützow* had been moved from their usual berths, *Tirpitz* was still immobile behind her nets, with an area of oil stretching two miles from the ship. Later, details of the damage were reported by Torstein Raaby.

That *Tirpitz* would be out of action for several months was evident enough. But she had not been sunk, and until she was sunk she would remain for the British a menace, and therefore a target. In time other means would have to be found to destroy her.

First indications that the attack by the X-craft on the *Tirpitz* had been successful came in this intercepted signal from the destroyer *Erich Steinbrinck* at Kaafjord to Naval Group North at Kiel. It was transmitted within two hours of the attack, and received, decrypted, at the Admiralty in the early afternoon of the following day.

22 September 1943

TOO   115?

FROM: BATTLE GROUP VIA 'STEINBRINCK'

TO: OPERATIONS DIVISION
GRUPPE NORD-FLOTTE

MOST IMMEDIATE

HEAVY EXPLOSION 60 METRES TO PORT OF 'TIRPITZ' AT 1012, (S/M DESTROYED BY TIME BOMBS.) 500 CUBIC METRES (OF WATER IN THE SHIP.) A SECOND S/M (WAS DESTROYED BY TIME BOMBS) 300 METRES (ON THE SHIP'S STARBOARD BOW) AT 1035. COMMANDING OFFICER WAS TAKEN PRISONER. A THIRD (S/M) WAS FIRED ON WHEN 600 METRES DISTANT ON THE STARBOARD BEAM, SEVERAL HITS BEING OBSERVED. (DEPT. NOTE: TEXT CORRUPT AND FRAGMENTARY BUT EMENDATIONS APPEAR JUSTIFIED. PASSED TO YOU AND THE DIRECTOR ONLY)

A somewhat puzzled inquiry from Naval Group North to *Tirpitz* as to how the midget submarines managed to penetrate the Kaafjord defences. This signal was sent on the day after the attack and reached the Admiralty, decrypted, the following afternoon.

23 September

TOO   2239

FROM: GRUPPE NORD-FLEET ((FLOTTE))

TO: BATTLE GROUP (ALSO TO OTHER ADDRESSEES)

EMERGENCY   MOST SECRET 03541 A 1

ROT:
1) WAS IT POSSIBLE FOR ENEMY SUBMARINES TO PENETRATE THROUGH OPEN BOOM GAP IN KAAFJORD AND BOOM GAP IN THE NET ENCLOSURE?
2) WERE BOOM GAPS OPENED BEFORE THE APPEARANCE OF THE SUBMARINES AND FOR HOW LONG?
3) WHAT IS THE NORMAL MANNER OF OPENING AND CLOSING THE BOOM GAPS?
4) IS THERE ANY EVIDENCE THAT THE SUBMARINES WENT THROUGH THE NET AND NOT THROUGH THE BOOM GAPS?

8. The Fleet Air Arm Strikes

But how was the *Tirpitz* to be repaired? How could the great wounds in her belly and sides be permanently healed? Dry-docking at Kiel or Wilhelmshaven was the obvious answer, but a passage there under tow, vulnerable for more than 1000 miles to attacks by enemy aircraft and submarines, was to invite further damage, even total destruction. To repair her without dry-dock facilities meant the introduction of techniques as yet untested; but when Herr Krux, director of German naval ship-repairing, reported the task to be feasible, Dönitz directed that *Tirpitz* was to make good her defects where she lay. With luck the British would not know of the extent of the defects, so her role as a fleet-in-being, a distant menace, could be maintained.

Accordingly the repair ship *Monte Rosa* and 800 German dockyard workmen arrived at Alta in early October, and at once set about repairs; many of *Tirpitz*'s crew were transferred to billets ashore. Repairs to the propeller shafts and port rudder were carried out by building a 100-foot-long coffer dam, securing it firmly to the ship's after sides and draining it of water; and the holes in the ship's bottom were sealed with underwater cement. As the long, cold winter nights lengthened, with only a few hours of daylight each day, most of the work was done by electric light, and elaborate security measures were enforced.

But from aerial reconnaissance and the reports of Torstein Raaby and others, sent by radio and to Captain Denham in Stockholm, it was evident it would be a long time before *Tirpitz* was seaworthy. The departure of the *Lützow* for Germany further weakened the northern battlegroup, and, with the *Scharnhorst* now the only fully operational fleet unit, the Cabinet felt able to restart the cycle of north Russian convoys.

The first two convoys reached their destinations without loss. During their passage *Scharnhorst* and her destroyers stayed at anchor in Altenfjord. In despair Admiral Kummetz, who as far back as March had been promised by Dönitz and Schniewind (Carls' successor at Naval Group North), an aggressive policy for the battlegroup, received permission to proceed to Germany on extended leave. His place was taken by the Commodore, Destroyers, Rear-Admiral Bey.

Yet Kummetz's departure was premature, for by mid-December, sensitive to the increasing reversal of arms being suffered by German land forces in Russia, Dönitz at last decided on surface action to relieve them. On Christmas Day 1943, Bey had joined Meyer for the usual Christmas lunch and to hear Meyer's address to the ship's company. There he received a signal from Schniewind to take the *Scharnhorst* to sea to operate against Convoy JW 55B, then in the area of Bear Island. At 7 p.m. that day *Scharnhorst* sailed. But Ultra intercepts of her intended movements and departure reached the British Admiralty within hours; and after three British cruisers had successfully prevented *Scharnhorst* from attacking the convoy, Admiral Fraser in the battleship *Duke of York* was able to cut off her return to the Norwegian coast. There, off the North Cape, she was sunk by the battleship's guns and destroyers' torpedoes. Of her crew of 1800 there were thirty-six survivors. Bey was not among them. Now the *Tirpitz* was alone.

The New Year dawned, and slowly the *Tirpitz* came back to life. On the night of 10–11 February she was attacked by Russian bombers but without success. Three weeks later her repairs were completed almost a month ahead of schedule, and on 15 March, after seven months of immobility in Kaafjord, she put to sea for exercises

ULTRA INTERCEPTS RELATING TO THE SINKING OF THE *SCHARNHORST* ON 26 DECEMBER 1943

25 December 1943

1. TOO   1056

   FROM: BATTLE GROUP

   MOST IMMEDIATE   MOST SECRET

   (OFFIZIER CYPHER)

   BATTLE GROUP IS TO BE AT 1 HOURS READINESS FROM 1300/25/12. 'SCHARNHORST' AND 4TH Z-FLOTILLA ARE TO ACKNOWLEDGE.

---

2. TOO   1527

   FROM: ADMIRAL NORTHERN WATERS

   TO: BATTLE GROUP
   ADMIRAL POLAR COAST

   MOST IMMEDIATE   MOST SECRET

   'OSTFRONT' 1700/25/12.

(The executive signal for the operation, code-named 'Ostfront', to start.)

---

26 December

3. TOO   0043

   ORDER FROM CAPT (U/B): DECYPHER IMMEDIATELY. FOR BOATS AT SEA ONLY.

   (OFFIZIER CYPHER)

   1) OWN BATTLE GROUP CONSISTING OF 'SCHARNHORST' AND 5 NEW DESTROYERS LEFT LOPPHAVET 2300/25 WITH THE INTENTION OF ATTACKING THE CONVOY AT ABOUT 0900/26.

4. TOO   1426

   FROM: CAPTAIN (U/B) NORWAY

                                    MOST SECRET

   BATTLE GROUP REPORTED AT 1240: AM IN ACTION
   WITH SEVERAL OPPONENTS IN AC 4133. RADAR
   GUNNERY BY HEAVY UNITS.

---

5. TOO   1656

   FROM: BATTLE GROUP

   TO: GRUPPE NORD-FLOTILLA

   MOST IMMEDIATE   MOST SECRET

   SQUARE AC 4677, HEAVY BATTLESHIP. AM IN
   ACTION.

---

6. TOO   1819

   FROM: 'SCHARNHORST'

   TO: GRUPPE NORD-FLOTTE

   MOST IMMEDIATE   MOST SECRET

   OPPONENT IS FIRING BY RADAR LOCATION AT MORE
   THAN 18,000 ((RANGE)). MY POSITION AC 4965,
   COURSE ((1))10 DEGREES, SPEED 26 KNOTS.

7. TOO   1802

   TO: ADMIRAL OF THE FLEET AND C. IN C.
   FLEET

   MOST IMMEDIATE   MOST SECRET

   SCHARNHORST WILL EVER REIGN SUPREME

   THE COMMANDING OFFICER

---

26 December

8. TOO   1945

   F.O. CRUISERS AND C.O. OF 'SCHARNHORST'
   REPORT AT 1825:

   TO: THE FUEHRER

                            MOST SECRET

   WE SHALL FIGHT TO THE LAST SHELL

---

9. TOO   1925

   FROM: SCHARNHORST

                            MOST SECRET

   AM STEERING FOR TANAFJORD. POSITION IS
   SQUARE AC 4992, SPEED 20 KNOTS.

   (DEPT. NOTE: THIS WAS THE LAST TRANSMISSION
   MADE BY SCHARNHORST)

---

27 December

10. TOO   0230

    FROM: 4TH DESTROYER FLOTILLA

    TO: TIRPITZ

                             MOST SECRET

    EMERGENCY

    PLEASE OPEN KAAFJORD BOOM AT 0500.

(On the day after the sinking of the *Scharnhorst*, her destroyers
return to Alta without her, and request *Tirpitz* to open the
Kaafjord boom.)

This intelligence soon reached the Admiralty, and new attacks were planned against her. And this time it was to be the turn of the Fleet Air Arm.

It may be wondered why, during her long period of immobility in Kaafjord, *Tirpitz* had remained unmolested by British bombers. But at this time the Royal Air Force possessed no bombers with the range to reach Altenfjord from British bases and return. Range was no problem for the navy's aircraft carriers, but their Swordfish and Albacores were designed as torpedo-carrying planes, and the bombs they did carry were not of sufficiently heavy calibre.

Now, however, a new naval aircraft had come into service, the Barracuda bomber. It could carry bombs of up to 1600 lb which, it was believed, could penetrate *Tirpitz*'s armoured deck if dropped from a height of not less than 3000 feet. Plans for a large-scale Barracuda attack were begun in December 1943 under the direction of Vice-Admiral Sir Henry Moore, Admiral Fraser's second-in-command. The attack was to consist of two strikes, an hour apart, with twenty-one Barracudas in each; these would be embarked in the fleet carriers *Victorious* and *Furious*. In addition, forty Corsair, Hellcat and Wildcat fighters would embark both in the fleet carriers and in the auxiliary carriers *Emperor, Pursuer* and *Searcher*. Their role was firstly to deal with enemy fighters and secondly, if not engaged, to strafe the *Tirpitz* with machine-gun fire before the air attack. A fifth carrier, *Fencer*, would provide the fleet with anti-submarine patrols and fighter defence.

Training was carried out in the early months of 1944, and culminated in a full-scale dummy exercise in Loch Eriboll in the far north of Scotland, where practice runs were made on a Home Fleet battleship, protected by a smokescreen and dummy batteries ashore. So well co-ordinated were the tactics that each attack lasted no more than a minute.

It was planned that all five carriers and their escorts should rendezvous 250 miles north-west of Altenfjord on 3 April, after two of the carriers had been released from covering the passage of the latest Russia-bound convoy JW 58, and that the attack would take place at first light on 4 April. But on 1 April Admiral Fraser, also covering the convoy in his battleship *Duke of York*, received an Ultra signal that full-speed trials that had been scheduled for *Tirpitz* that day had been postponed until the 3rd. This told him two things: that JW 58 was no longer in need of carrier protection from surface attack, and that *Tirpitz* would be most vulnerable leaving Kaafjord, when she would be without the benefit of smoke canisters and the flak posts ashore. He therefore detached the two carriers from JW 58, and advanced the time of the operation by twenty-four hours.

By the afternoon of the 2nd all the carriers were in company and steaming towards the fly-off position 120 miles north-west of Kaafjord. That evening the Barracuda wings took on their bombs: ten with one armour-piercing bomb of 1600 lb; twenty-two with three 500 lb bombs, semi-armour-piercing; and ten with one 600 lb bomb for underwater blast effect. At 1.30 a.m. on the 3rd the air crews were roused from a brief sleep, given a bacon and egg breakfast, and assembled for a final briefing. Few slept soundly or ate much breakfast. 'We were told it was going to be a very dangerous attack,' said one pilot, 'and that we must expect heavy casualties.' The engines of the planes, now ranged on the flight-deck, had been warmed up by the deck crews, and pilots, observers and air-gunners clambered in. Just before take-off Admiral Fraser received a further Ultra signal that *Tirpitz* would be leaving her berth at 5.30 a.m. It looked like the perfect moment for attack.

At 4.30 a.m. the first strike of twenty-one Barracudas and forty Corsairs, Hellcats and Wildcats took off and headed south, flying at sea level to avoid enemy radar.

Twenty-five miles from the coast they climbed to 8000 feet to clear the mountains. 'It was the most beautiful morning,' said Sub-Lieutenant Russell Jones, 'a cloudless sky, the sea dead calm, and the snow on the mountains glowing pink in the morning sun. You could see for what seemed hundreds of miles.' By 5.15 a.m. they were only twenty miles from their target. They passed over a high mountain, 'and there,' said Sub-Lieutenant Roy Eveleigh, 'at the head of the fjord just where intelligence told us she would be, lay the *Tirpitz*, looking as large as life and very forbidding.'

No enemy fighters having appeared, the commander of the British fighter wing radioed, 'Out lights!' This was the signal for them to assume their secondary role of strafing the *Tirpitz* with machine-gun fire, destroying the radar and flak control and killing all those in exposed positions on deck, thus demoralising and confusing the enemy before the main attack. They screamed down on the battleship from every side and raked her superstructure from stem to stern. 'Some of my ammunition was red tracer,' said Sub-Lieutenant Laurie Brander, 'and I well remember seeing it strike the *Tirpitz*'s armour plating, then bouncing up into the sky and disappearing.'

Next came the Barracudas, and in their relief at finding no fighter opposition they dived down to well below 3000 feet, ignoring the small brown puffs of the anti-aircraft shells exploding around them, determined to obtain a hit at all costs. The circling British fighters not engaged in strafing other ships or flak posts in the fjord saw the bombs hit their target, licks of flame shooting upwards, dark brown smoke rising from aft, fountains of white water erupting alongside. The whole attack took only one minute; then the planes were gone, jinking their way seawards. Only one Barracuda was lost.

An hour later came the second strike, and the pattern was repeated. By now the smokescreen from the canisters ashore had enveloped the anchorage, but for *Tirpitz* this was counter-productive: while the outlines of the battle-ship were perfectly visible to the British pilots, the smoke obscured the vision of the German gunners. Again the fighters raked bridge, aerials, radar and flak crews with machine-gun fire, again the Barracudas came in low to drop their bombs and again after just one minute the planes had disappeared and the fjord was silent. Again, too, only one Barracuda was lost.

For the men of *Tirpitz*, the morning that had dawned so full of promise and beauty – high-speed trials in the sunlit fjords – ended in tragedy. The first attack could not have come at a worse moment, just as the anchors were coming in and the tugs standing by to tow the ship clear of the nets. The time was 5.29 a.m., or just one minute earlier than that promulgated in the Ultra intercept.

By 5.31 a.m., after the first strike, the upper decks of the *Tirpitz* were a shambles, with more than a hundred men dead, including the senior surgeon Dr Gombert, and more than 200 wounded, including Captain Meyer, who had to be relieved by Commander Junge. Some had had lucky escapes. As the alarm bells rang, Lieutenant Kühnen was in his cabin bending down to pick up a packet of cigarettes. A second later machine-gun bullets tore through the porthole and into the mirror before which he had been standing. At least fourteen bombs had caused serious damage; destruction of the flak control and bridge telegraphs; fires in the aircraft hangar, wardroom, gunroom, mess decks and a store room; buckling of the keel plates and underwater flooding. In the second attack there were hits on the fo'c'sle, upper decks, hangar and a gun turret. The final casualties were 122 killed and 316 wounded. The only consolation for the Germans was that none of the bombs had penetrated the armoured deck, so engine and boiler rooms were unharmed and the ship was still seaworthy. Had the Barracudas kept to their ordered dropping height of 3000 feet – from which the 1600 lb bombs had the momentum to penetrate armour – the damage must have been even greater.

That morning the Admiralty learned of the success of the attack from an Ultra intercept timed 7.13 a.m. A few days later a more detailed account of the damage arrived from Torstein Raaby: 'Ambulances were driving to and fro for two days. On *Tirpitz* we can count five holes in the deck on the port side. She has a list to starboard. A lot of scrap iron brought ashore and taken to the bay. Officers mess and galley received a direct hit. On Monday they cooked food on the beach. Germans say *Tirpitz* will be out of action for several months.' The triumphant carrier force returned to Scapa Flow, and *Tirpitz* retired once again behind her nets to lick her wounds, bury her dead, and signal for replacements for her decimated guncrews.

From the reports of Raaby the British concluded that it would be at least six months before *Tirpitz* could again become operational. In fact it took her only three months, during which further defensive measures were taken against aircraft attack. Radar installations on the coast were improved, the smokescreen apparatus was strengthened, and an observation post was set up on top of a nearby hill from which, by direct line to the ship, Sub-Lieutenant Brunner could co-ordinate anti-aircraft fire, including that from the battleship's 15-inch guns. Yet the most pressing need for *Tirpitz*'s defence always had been and always would be German fighter planes, but because of the lack of co-operation between the German Navy and the Luftwaffe they never came.

After the successful Fleet Air Arm attack Dönitz decided that *Tirpitz*'s sea-going days were finally at an end; the enemy's naval air strength was now such as to preclude attacks on Arctic convoys. Her role in the future would be as a floating battery in defence of Norway against the invasion that Hitler believed imminent. Had the British known of this, they would have been spared much worry, expense and effort. Several more Fleet Air Arm sorties were launched against her, but all failed either because of the weather or the effectiveness of the smoke-screen. In one, on 24 August, a 1600 lb bomb did succeed in penetrating the armoured deck and ended up in a lower deck switchroom, having failed to explode. 'Had it exploded,' writes one historian, 'it would have wrecked the fire control room and caused serious flooding, so that *Tirpitz* would have been rendered useless, if not actually sunk.' When the bomb was defused, it was found to contain less than half its allotted amount of explosive.

For Winston Churchill and the British Admiralty, *Tirpitz*'s continued stubborn existence was now as much of a nuisance as a menace: it was unlikely she would become operational again, but the possibility remained. The chariots, the X-craft, the Fleet Air Arm had all failed to sink her. What remained? The answer this time was the Royal Air Force; coupled with the names of Dr Barnes Wallis and his huge Tallboy bomb.

9. Tallboy

Dr Barnes Wallis was fifty-three when war broke out, an aircraft designer by trade, and described as 'having the air of a diffident and gentle cleric'. He had been designing since the end of the First War, and was responsible for the airships R-100 and R-101, later the Wellington bomber. From the beginning of the war he became convinced that the standard 500 lb bomb then in use was far too small and ineffective; what he wanted was a bomb weighing several tons, a plane specially adapted to carry it, and a precision bomb-sight.

It took Dr Wallis nearly three years and several treatises before his ideas were accepted. His first big bomb, a 3-tonner, was designed to breach German dams. Successful experiments led to the formation of the famous No 617 'Dam-buster' squadron which in 1943, under Wing-Commander Guy Gibson, burst the walls of the Moehne and Eder dams, releasing millions of tons of water into the countryside. Air Marshal Sir Arthur Harris, Chief of Bomber Command, was so impressed that he persuaded Wallis to design a 6-ton bomb, to be fitted in converted Lancasters, for attacking the German secret weapons sites. Thus was born the famous 21-foot-long Tallboy or 'earthquake' bomb, so constructed that it would gain speed as it fell and penetrate the earth to some eighty feet before exploding. It was deployed with shattering effect on various targets in northern France and Germany, and now it was decided to use it against the *Tirpitz*.

Thirty-six Lancaster bombers from Nos 617 and 9 squadrons under the command of Wing-Commander J. B. Tait, a much decorated officer, were detailed for the attack. But as the planes, with their heavy loads, did not have the range to reach Altenfjord and return, it was agreed with the Russians that they would fly first to an airfield on an island at Yagodnik near Archangel, deliver the attack from there, return to Yagodnik for refuelling, and thence fly to the United Kingdom. An attack from the east would have the added advantage of surprise.

The planes left Woodhall Spa in Lincolnshire on 11 September. Thirty eventually reached Yagodnik next day, but six lost themselves over unfamiliar territory, force-landed and had to be abandoned. The British aircrews were accommodated in a houseboat, draped with a banner which read: 'Welcome to the glorious flyers of the Royal Air Force.' For three rainy days they were entertained with vodka, Russian war films and a football match, which the Russian aircrews won 7–0; they also suffered from mosquitoes and bed bugs.

On 15 September, on receipt of a favourable weather report, twenty-seven of the Lancasters, led by Tait, took off for the attack, approaching from the south-east. At first they flew low, not more than 1000 feet, then for the sixty miles run-in to the target they climbed to over 12,000 feet. Thirty miles away the leading planes sighted *Tirpitz*, 'sitting under its cliff', said one pilot, 'just as we'd been shown on the model'. They saw the flash of the battleship's big guns opening up on them and the smokescreen forming round the fjord. By the time they were over the target three minutes later the smokescreen had almost obliterated it. But not quite: for a brief last moment the tip of her foremast came into the sights of Tait's bomb-aimer, Daniels.

'Bomb sights on,' he shouted.

Away went Tait's bomb, and seconds later the bombs of most of the rest of the squadron, aimed at random into the centre of the thick blanket of smoke. Some of the last planes did not release their bombs, having no aiming point at all. When they returned to Yagodnik they claimed no hits, though all hoped that a lucky one had found its mark.

In fact they had been luckier than they knew, for Tait's bomb had struck *Tirpitz* on the bows with devastating effect, passing through the ship's side and exploding beneath the keel. A great hole had been blown in the fo'c'sle, 30 feet deep by 50 feet long, letting in some 1000 tons of water. 'The hole is both above and below the water-line,' reported Torstein Raaby, 'and is so large that a big motor-boat could go in.' There had also been two near misses. The armoured deck had been wrecked, the main engines put out of action, and many of the fire-control instruments again destroyed.

Tirpitz had now been crippled for life, and Captain Wolf Junge (who had been Meyer's second-in-command and succeeded him in May) proposed to Dönitz that she be taken out of service. But Dönitz still believed she had a role to play as a floating battery, no longer in the north where Russian troops were now threatening Finmark, but at Tromsö, 200 miles to the south, where, despite the Normandy invasion in June, Hitler still believed a secondary attack might come.

On 15 October, with her bows temporarily patched up, *Tirpitz* left Kaafjord for the last time. Steaming at 7 knots, and escorted by every available warship in northern waters, she made her way south through the leads, arriving at Tromsö next day. A special berth had been prepared for her in the lee of Haaköy Island, three miles from Tromsö. Here the water was so shallow that it was considered that even if she was sunk in another air attack she would still be able to fire her guns to seawards while resting on the bottom. She brought her anti-torpedo nets and smoke canisters with her, and a squadron of fighters – for which every previous captain had pressed in vain – was posted to nearby Bardufoss airfield to protect her.

Her arrival at Tromsö was first reported by Egil Lindberg, a Norwegian agent operating from an attic in the town's mortuary, and confirmed soon after by a Mosquito reconnaissance plane. For the British this was a stroke of luck, for it meant that with suitable modifications to the Lancasters they would now have sufficient fuel to attack the ship from British bases and return. Accordingly the two squadrons that had made the attack from Russia had their mid-upper gun turrets and cockpit armour removed, extra fuel tanks installed, and the existing engines replaced with more powerful ones.

The removal of the gun turrets and the armour inevitably made the aircrews more vulnerable to attack by the fighters at Bardufoss, whose arrival had been reported to British intelligence; and as the British had also learned from an Ultra signal to German military attachés abroad that the ship was no longer operational, it may be wondered why so many lives should have been risked and so much effort expended in attacking a target that had now ceased to threaten them. Perhaps, like Everest, she had to be conquered because she was there; perhaps it was a matter of pride, that past failures had to be redeemed by ultimate success.

In the early hours of 29 October, thirty-two Lancasters, again under Tait, took off from Lossiemouth to make a further attack. They concentrated over a lake in Sweden, then formed up for their run-in to the target. But the weather was against them, with drifting clouds below the 13,000 feet at which they were scheduled to attack. Nevertheless they made several runs over the target and dropped their bombs. There was no sign of German fighters. All the planes returned except one which, damaged by flak, force-landed in Sweden.

One of the Tallboys, a near miss, had in fact caused considerable further damage, distorting the port propeller shaft and rudder and resulting in flooding along more than 100 feet of the port side aft. This meant the ship could no longer steam under her own power, and on Junge's recommendation her complement of 2000 was reduced by some 400 men – mostly engine-room staff, as the engines were now required only to make steam for the generators and domestic services. The craters made by the Tallboys in the sea-bed had also revealed that the bottom consisted of mud, not, as had been thought, rock, and to prevent the ship capsizing in another air attack it was arranged for tons of rubble to be dumped by dredgers below her keel.

Topp's once proud *Tirpitz* was now a partial wreck, flooded fore and aft, powerless to move, no longer functioning as a weapon either of offence or defence. Her crew, listening to the daily radio bulletins from Germany, with reports of continued advances by the Russians in the east and the Allies in the west, knew the war was as good as lost, and wondered what possible service was left to them to perform. They knew that sooner or later the big four-engine bombers would return, and go on returning until they had completed their task. 'God help us,' thought Captain Junge, 'if one of those block-busters hits us.'

Junge himself was under orders to relinquish his command for an appointment in Berlin. He asked for the order to be countermanded for the sake of the crew. His request was refused and he left the ship on 4 November 1944. His successor was Captain Robert Weber, the ship's former gunnery officer, who had delighted the wardroom with his imitations of Hitler at the 1942 New Year's Eve party in Foettenfjord.

In Britain, meanwhile, it had been decided that any further attacks against *Tirpitz* would have to be made before the end of November; after that, in the high latitude of Tromsö, there would not be enough light, even at midday, for high-level precision bombing. Bad weather over Norway prevailed throughout late October and early November, but on 11 November Wing-Commander Tait was playing a game of football with his aircrews when he was summoned to the office of his chief, Air Vice Marshal Ralph Cochrane. He appeared as he was, in striped jersey and studded boots.

'The weather forecast is good for Tromsö,' said Cochrane, 'we want you to go.'

'When, sir?'

'Now.'

That night the Lancasters and their Tallboys assembled again at Lossiemouth. It was a cold, clear, frosty night. At 2.30 a.m. on the 12th the engines of thirty-nine Lancasters were started up, and soon the darkened airfield was reverberating to their deafening roar. At 3 a.m. the first plane became airborne. Thirty-one others followed. Seven had icing problems and were unable to take off.

Through the night the Lancasters flew independently across the North Sea. The crews were in optimistic mood, believing that this would be third time lucky – though a few had nagging doubts about the German fighters, knowing that if they did appear they must expect heavy casualties. At dawn they were over Norway. 'It was the most beautiful morning,' said one pilot, 'mountains and snow and frozen lakes as far as you could see.' Once again the assembly area was the lake in Sweden, and one by one the big, black bombers arrived there, formed up into their allotted groups and, with Tait leading, set course for Tromsö.

On board the *Tirpitz* the day had started much as usual. The hands were called, colours hoisted and working parties detailed for cleaning and maintenance. Lieutenant-Commander Kühnen and Sub-Lieutenant Brunner went across to Haaköy in a boat to supervise the building of a landing stage. Lieutenant Schmitz, who had just returned from surveying a new berth for *Tirpitz* that might give her greater natural protection (the anchorage off Haaköy was quite exposed), was having breakfast in the wardroom before reporting to the captain. Ashore the engineer officer, Lieutenant-Commander Sommer, was waiting for a boat to take him to the ship.

It was about 7.30 a.m. when Captain Weber received the first reports of enemy aircraft, a long way south, and apparently heading in the direction of Sweden. The anti-aircraft officer, Lieutenant-Commander Fassbender, was informed, and alerted his own officers. At 8.15 a further report was received of three Lancasters over Mosjoen, still a long way away, but coming in *Tirpitz*'s direction. Captain Weber asked his signals officer to get through to Bardufoss immediately and inform Major Erler, in command of the fighters; once airborne they could be over the ship in ten minutes. Then he ordered action stations and the hoisting of the blue and yellow aircraft alarm flag – the signal for the few batteries stationed on Haaköy and around Tromsö to prepare for aircraft attack.

Weber and other officers, among them his executive officer, Commander Muller, Lieutenant Schmitz, the signals officer, and the chaplain, Pastor Seeberg, went to the bridge. It was a clear, calm, cloudless day, the water smooth as glass, not a breath of wind anywhere, perfect conditions for attack. There were no high hills to hide *Tirpitz*, as there had been in Foettenfjord and Kaafjord, and the smoke canisters, though positioned, had not yet been primed. *Tirpitz* was as naked as if she had been at sea.

Time went by without further news. The ship was quite silent. Everyone waited quietly at their action stations, at the guns large and small, in the wireless room and communications centre amidships, at the rangefinders and radar post in the foretop, in the switchboard rooms and magazines far below. Then at long last, through the forward rangefinders, the planes were sighted, seventy kilometres away to the south-east, tiny, black insects, more than thirty of them, flying in tiered formation in groups of three and four, relentless in their approach. But where were Major Erler's fighters? The signals officer got through to Bardufoss again, and was told they had taken off.

At 9.38 a.m., when the Lancasters were some fifteen miles away, Captain Weber gave orders for the main armament to open fire. A and B turrets opened up first, then C and D turrets in barrage fire, their blast shaking the whole ship, deafening in their concerted roar. Then the high-angle anti-aircraft guns joined in; and puffs of brown smoke could be seen as the shells burst high up in the clear sky. But they made no difference to the bombers, which came resolutely on. Captain Weber and the bridge party entered the armoured conning-tower. Before they closed the overhead hatch they saw the first of the Tallboys leave the planes and, gathering speed, begin their descent towards them.

Others, too, saw the bombs fall – Kühnen and Brunner ashore at the landing stage, Sommer waiting for his boat, farmers on Haaköy, people in Tromsö who had been forewarned of the attack by the increasing drone of the Lancasters' approach. With a roar that shook the town and broke windows in houses half a mile away the bombs landed, enveloping *Tirpitz* in a curtain of splashes that rose as high as her mainmast, a blend of water and mud. One bomb hit B turret, another struck amidships, penetrating the armoured deck before exploding, two others landed on the port side, opened up the ship's side as though with a can-opener, tore a great hole in her that let in thousands of tons of water.

'Oh, I should think we could see the Tirpitz *from about 30 miles out. Gin-clear sky and we could see the ship sitting there naked and we knew we were going to get her. As we neared the target, everyone was opening their bomb doors, and the gaggle was still complete – we'd forgotten all about the fighters they warned us about. Over the target we could see the bombs of the other aircraft going down – you can't really see your own bomb going down, only the other ones. They were mighty close – and the splashes were tremendous – even at 15,000 feet they seemed to be, coming right up at us. Then our bomb-aimer shouted, "We've hit her", and I was so pleased, and we went into orbit to try and see what damage had been done. And then to our delight we saw her gradually going over – though her guns were still firing which impressed us very much. We knew we'd got her then. It made our day.'*

Extract from an interview with Terry Playford from the BBC Television documentary 'Target Tirpitz'.

he attack lasted just three minutes. Then there was near
.ence, the only sound the diminishing drone of the
ancasters as they headed seawards for home. As the
noke cleared, the watchers on shore saw that the ship had
ken on a list to port. At about 20 degrees it seemed to be
ecked. Then, without warning, the after 15-inch maga-
ne blew up, lifting C turret and her crew, weighing over
)00 tons, bodily into the air, hurling it into the water
rty yards away and, sending up a huge column of smoke.
mong her dead was Sub-Lieutenant Leine who, a year
:fore, had tried to capture X-6 in *Tirpitz*'s launch.

Now, as the attention of those on shore returned to the
ip, it was noticed that the list to port which had seemed
 be checked was increasing. Slowly, very slowly, it
emed, the ship leaned further and further over, until the
arboard keel plates began to show one side and the
pperworks were level with the water on the other. For a
oment she lay motionless on her side, then as more and
ore water poured into her torn compartments she turned
ght over until her upperworks touched the bottom and all
at could be seen on the surface was her long, shiny keel,
ke a stranded whale. At long last *Tirpitz*'s life had ended.

But what had happened to her company? How many of
em had died, how many were still alive, trapped in the
pturned hull?

Commander Sommer's boat would never come now, so
e commandeered another and set out for the ship;
aptain Krüger, the senior German naval officer ashore at
romsö, organised others to follow. When they arrived an
our later, they found hundreds of men, some wounded,
wimming in the oily water near the hull, others clinging to
e anti-torpedo netting that surrounded the ship. Among
ese was Lieutenant Bernard Schmitz, still wearing his
ap; he was the only survivor from the armoured conning-
ower, having escaped through a hatch to the chartroom
ist as the ship was beginning to turn turtle and Captain
/eber had given the order to evacuate below decks. The

doors of the conning-tower, he said, were alread
jammed, so the captain and bridge party had all bee
trapped.

'While I was eating in the mess, the sirens went, warning us of
coming air attack. I went to the bridge and was told that a larg
bomber squadron had been sighted. At about 8.30 I could see th
planes, 28 or 30 Lancasters, through the bridge telescope. Soo
after, our 15-inch guns opened fire. We went into the armoure
tower. Then the bombs began to drop. One hit the ship forwar
and another near the funnel. I stood on the starboard side an
tried to balance myself by holding on to the gas-mask rack. Bu
the ship shook so violently with the explosions that I suddenl
found the rack in my hand, the brackets had torn loose from th
armour plating.

'The ship was already listing to port. The signals officer ordere
me to open one of the armoured doors, but it had got jammed,
was impossible. I tried the other side but that door was jamme
too. I was given permission to go down to the chartroom whic
was my proper action station. The captain and other officer
decided to stay in the tower so long as the guns were firing. On m
way down the men asked me if there was any chance of the shi
turning over. I told them it was impossible, we did not hav
enough water under the bottom. I must have been the last perso
to see the captain alive.

'When I reached the deck, I saw the masts and main turre
coming towards me. I didn't want to get buried under all th
debris so I jumped into the water and swam away as fast as
could. I was still wearing my seaboots and full kit. Around m
were a lot of men with their arms held high, and I saw them sink i
front of my eyes which was a terrible sight. I swam about 15
metres to the anti-torpedo nets and reached a buoy. Turnin
round, I saw the ship had listed over even further, to about 13
degrees. The torpedo tubes were level with the water. I don'
know how long I stayed there, but it must have been one and
half to two hours. My watch and my cufflinks were the only thing
I saved.

'I lay in hospital for a few days after that, and was overcom
for the first time with a deep depression. The ship had been ou
home. I had felt secure on board her, and I would have liked t
stay with her. Now we had lost our home, and for the first time
became clear to me that this dreadful war, which I had hope

138

would have a satisfactory ending, was for us finally lost too.'

xtract from an interview with Bernard Schmitz from the BBC Television
Documentary 'Target Tirpitz'.

But Sommer's concern was with the hundreds of men who must be still inside the hull, some of whom might even now be working their way upwards through the various compartments. The only way to fetch them out was by burning holes in the upturned keel. The repair ship *Neumark* had blow-lamps in plenty, but unfortunately had gone to sea. He sent a Norwegian boat back to Tromsö to round up any blow-lamps that could be found, and to bring spades and sand to give a foothold on the slippery, barnacled keel. But he knew it would be a long time before they could start work.

The action station of Sub-Lieutenant Heinz Bernstein, who had been in the *Tirpitz* since she commissioned, was in the main switchboard control-room, down in the bowels of the ship, only three decks from the bottom. When the attack started he and his party were aware of a great deal of noise and vibration but couldn't tell the difference between the firing of the ship's guns and the explosion of the bombs. As the ship began listing he reported to the bridge that he no longer had communication with the engine-room and two switchboards, and soon after he received the order to evacuate. Then the lights went out, and in the darkness his party found they could no longer stand upright; they were slithering sideways on to the bulkhead, loose gear was crashing about them. When the emergency lights came on they saw the control panel was upside down; the deck of the control-room was now above them. From the former deckhead on which they were now standing water was seeping in. The ship was upside down.

Their only chance of escape was to go upwards, towards

the keel which, they hoped, was above the surface of the water. They climbed the ladder to No 3 switchroom (normally below them), on the way finding oxygen bottles and breathing apparatus which they gratefully seized. Here they heard knocking on the bulkhead, and having managed to open the door leading to No 3 generator-room they were joined by another thirty-two men.

Between them and what they hoped was the sky was only the ship's double-bottom, a dark cavernous space that normally held fuel oil, but which thankfully they knew had been drained. They managed to unscrew the manhole that gave access to it, and were assailed by the stench of gases. One by one they hoisted themselves through. Now there was only the hull above them, but rescue could only come from outside. Would anyone in fact come? Or was this where they were going to die?

To conserve energy Bernstein ordered the party to lie down in the sludge and for those with torches to switch them off. There was no sound from above. At intervals men were detailed to tap on the hull with spanners, but no answer came. It was bitterly cold. Soon the air became so foul that some men felt dizzy, as though about to lose consciousness. Bernstein ordered one of the precious oxygen bottles to be opened, and the air revived them a little. They took it in turns to sleep and tap. Morning gave way to afternoon. The men became weaker. Another oxygen bottle was opened. They went on tapping. No answer came.

In another part of the ship, further forward, Seaman Gerlach had been at his action station in the transmission centre, below the armoured deck. Gerlach first realised the ship was heeling over when he saw his fiancée's photograph slide off the desk. The fuses in the control panel went out one by one, then, as the ship heeled further, the fuse boxes broke loose from the bulkheads. He and his companion decided it was time to go.

At first they believed their best hope of escape was

upwards, towards the main deck, but when they reached the bandsmen's mess and found mess-tables and benches, instruments and rifles, lying on the deckhead, and the place filling with water, they realised they must go back the way they had come. Five other men joined them, then the lights went out. The water rose rapidly and was soon up to their thighs. There seemed to be no way out. One man had a revolver and they discussed whether to shoot each other, but were unable to decide who should do it. Then Gerlach remembered he had a torch, and though it was in his trouser pocket, underwater, he was able to switch it on. By the light of the torch they swam to a watertight door, opened it, and eventually found a ladder leading upwards, towards the bottom, which took them out of the water. They reached the forward refrigerator room, then the machine-shop, where they found twelve other men. Above them was the forward double-bottom, but unlike Bernstein's party they were unable to undo the manhole leading into it. So they stood on the deckhead of the machine-shop and began tapping.

In Bernstein's double-bottom they had been tapping for hours, more to keep them occupied than anything else. Some had almost given up hope of rescue, were resigning themselves to death. Then, unexpectedly, came the sounds of which they had been dreaming, footsteps marching on the hull, answering taps from above.

Everyone stood up, looked, waited. Soon the red tip of a blow-lamp showed in the steel hull, and molten metal began falling into the tank. Now there was a danger of fire, of explosion of the gases, but it was a risk that had to be taken. A small fire did start, but was put out immediately with an extinguisher. There was a small hissing sound as the fresh air entered the tank, and then a circular plate of one-inch steel crashed inwards, and there was the sky above.

'Sommer here!' said a voice they all knew, 'who's down here?'

141

'Bernstein and thirty-six others.'

'We'll soon have you out.'

The exhausted men were brought up one by one, put into boats and taken ashore. Gerlach's party were rescued in the same way, and all through the night Sommer's rescue party drilled more holes in the hull to search for others. Next day more tapping was heard very faintly, and another party of six men were brought up, one so near to madness that he refused to leave the ship and had to be forcibly removed. Contact was also made with another group of three, Sub-Lieutenant Mettegang, Sturm, Dieckmann, trapped in an air-pocket below the water-line; but it needed special equipment, which they did not have, to reach them, and they had to be left to die.

Altogether eighty-seven men were taken from the hull. Six hundred were rescued from the water, and some 900 were killed, drowned, or suffocated on board.

Before the Lancasters turned for home they had seen the ship beginning to turn over, and believed their mission had been accomplished at last. That night Emil Lindberg, transmitting from the attic of the mortuary, which even then was receiving *Tirpitz*'s dead, sent out a signal confirming it. But it failed to reach London. Next day a Mosquito reconnaissance plane flew over the anchorage and reported by radio that from visual observation it looked as though *Tirpitz* had capsized. Before the plane had landed and its photographs could be developed, Commander Denning in the Admiralty rang up Bletchley to see if there had been any relevant Ultra intercepts the day before. And sure enough one was found: 'From Naval Communications Officer Tromsö to Naval Group North, Flag Officer Norway. *Tirpitz* blown up and capsized. 0946/12/44.'

Epilogue

Such was the story of the battleship *Tirpitz*. Her career, unlike that of her sister *Bismarck*, which was brief and glorious, was long and pitiful. It was true that she had fulfilled a useful role as a fleet-in-being, tying down enemy forces that might have been used elsewhere. But in the last analysis wars are won by aggressive, not passive, action.

Neither in calibre of ships nor morale of men was the German Navy inferior to that of the British – only in the lack of resolution with which Hitler constrained the High Command. *Tirpitz* arrived too late on the scene to influence the Battle of the Atlantic; but had her flag officers, Ciliax, Schniewind and Kummetz, been encouraged to attack the Arctic convoys with the same skill and initiative of the U-boat captains, even at the risk of loss, then the war in the Arctic might have been transformed. The destruction by surface forces of only one convoy and its escorts would not only have done wonders for morale in the fleet and at home; it would have gone far towards persuading the British Admiralty that such convoys were no longer an acceptable risk, and so directly helped their comrades on the eastern front. As it was, a great ship built for the destruction of her enemies lived an invalid's life and died a cripple's death.

For a long time afterwards the ugly hulk remained where it lay. After the war the Norwegian government sold her to a salvage company, and over the years they picked her carcass clean. Today, thirty-five years later, all that remains of the last of Hitler's battleships are a few pieces of rusty iron lying on a quiet beach.

BATTLESHIPS OF THE SECOND WORLD WAR

Name	Completion year (re-building completion in brackets)	Tonnage	GUNS Main	GUNS Secondary	GUNS Heavy AA	Speed in knots	Armour (maximum thickness of side belt in inches)
BRITAIN							
Old battleships							
Queen Elizabeth	1915(1941)	31,000	8 15-in	20 4·5-in DP		24	13
Valiant	1916(1939)	31,000	8 15-in	20 4·5-in DP		24	13
Warspite	1915(1937)	31,000	8 15-in	8 6-in	8 4-in	24	13
Barham	1915	31,000	8 15-in	12 6-in	8 4-in	25	13
Malaya	1916	31,000	8 15-in	12 6-in	8 4-in	25	13
Revenge	1916	29,000	8 15-in	12 6-in	8 4-in	22	13
Resolution	1916	29,000	8 15-in	12 6-in	8 4-in	22	13
Royal Oak	1916	29,000	8 15-in	12 6-in	8 4-in	22	13
Royal Sovereign	1916	29,000	8 15-in	12 6-in	8 4-in	22	13
Ramillies	1917	29,000	8 15-in	12 6-in	8 4-in	22	13
Renown	1916(1939)	32,000	6 15-in	20 4·5-in DP		29	9
Repulse	1916	32,000	6 15-in	9 4-in	8 4-in	30	9
Hood	1920	41,000	8 15-in	12 5·5-in	8 4-in	31	12

N.B. The *Renown*, *Repulse* and *Hood* were classified as battlecruisers.

Intermediate type

Nelson	1927	34,000	9 6-in	12 6-in	8 4·7-in	23	14
Rodney	1927	34,000	9 16-in	12 6-in	8 4·7-in	23	14

Fast battleships

King George V	1940	38,000	10 14-in	16 5·25-in DP		27	15
Prince of Wales	1941	38,000	10 14-in	16 5·25-in DP		27	15
Duke of York	1941	38,000	10 14-in	16 5·25-in DP		27	15
Howe	1942	38,000	10 14-in	16 5·25-in DP		27	15
Anson	1942	38,000	10 14-in	16 5·25-in DP		27	15

FRANCE

Old battleships

Courbet	1913	22,000	12 12-in	22 5·5-in	5 2·9-in	20	10½
Paris	1914	22,000	12 12-in	22 5·5-in	7 2·9-in	20	10½
Provence	1915(1923/27/33)	22,000	10 13·4-in	14 5·5-in	8 2·9-in	21	10½
Bretagne	1915(1921/25/34)	22,000	10 13·4-in	14 5·5-in	8 2·9-in	21	10½
Lorraine	1916(1922/27/36)	21,500	10 13·4-in	14 5·5-in	8 2·9-in	21	10½

Name	Completion year (re-building completion in brackets)	Tonnage	GUNS			Speed in knots	Armour (maximum thickness of side belt in inches)
			Main	Secondary	Heavy AA		
Fast battleships							
Dunkerque	1937	27,000	8 13-in	16 5·1-in DP		29	9½
Strasbourg	1938	27,000	8 13-in	16 5·1-in DP		29	9½
Richelieu	1940	39,000	8 15-in	9 6-in	12 3·9-in	30	13
Jean Bart	1955	43,000	8 15-in	9 6-in	12 3·9-in	30	13

N.B. The *Jean Bart* was in action against US ships thirteen years before completion.

GERMANY

Old battleships							
Schlesien	1908(1927)	12,000	4 11-in	10 5·9-in	4 3·5-in	18	9½
Schleswig-Holstein	1908(1926)	12,000	4 11-in	10 5·9-in	4 3·5-in	18	9½
Special type							
Lützow	1933	12,000	6 11-in	8 5·9-in	6 3·9-in	26	2½
Admiral Scheer	1934	12,000	6 11-in	8 5·9-in	6 3·9-in	26	2½
Admiral Graf Spee	1936	12,500	6 11-in	8 5·9-in	6 4·1-in	26	3

GERMANY—continued

Fast battleships

Gneisenau	1938	32,000	9 11-in	12 5·9-in	14 4·1-in	31	14
Scharnhorst	1939	32,000	9 11-in	12 5·9-in	14 4·1-in	31	14
Bismarck	1940	42,000	8 15-in	12 5·9-in	16 4·1-in	29	12½
Tirpitz	1941	42,000	8 15-in	12 5·9-in	16 4·1-in	29	12½

ITALY

Old battleships

Giulio Cesare	1914(1937)	24,000	10 12·6-in	12 4·7-in	8 3·9-in	28	10
Conte di Cavour	1915(1937)	24,000	10 12·6-in	12 4·7-in	8 3·9-in	28	10
Caio Duillio	1915(1940)	24,000	10 12·6-in	12 5·3-in	10 3·6-in	28	10
Andrea Doria	1916(1940)	24,000	10 12·6-in	12 5·3-in	10 3·6-in	28	10

Fast battleships

Vittorio Veneto	1940	41,000	9 15-in	12 6-in	12 3·6-in	30	14
Italia	1940	41,000	9 15-in	12 6-in	12 3·6-in	30	14
Roma	1942	41,000	9 15-in	12 6-in	12 3·6-in	30	14

Name	Completion year (re-building completion in brackets)	Tonnage	GUNS			Speed in knots	Armour (maximum thickness of side belt in inches)
			Main	Secondary	Heavy AA		
JAPAN							
Old battleships							
Kongo	1913(1937)	32,000	8 14-in	14 6-in	8 5-in	30	9
Hiei	1914(1940)	32,000	8 14-in	14 6-in	4 5-in	30	9
Haruna	1915(1934)	32,000	8 14-in	14 6-in	8 5-in	30	9
Kirishima	1915(1936)	32,000	8 14-in	14 6-in	8 5-in	30	9
Fuso	1915(1935)	35,000	12 14-in	14 6-in	8 5-in	24	12
Yamashiro	1917(1935)	35,000	12 14-in	14 6-in	8 5-in	24	12
Ise	1917(1937)	36,000	12 14-in	16 5·5-in	8 5-in	25	12
Hyuga	1918(1934)	36,000	12 14-in	16 5·5-in	8 5-in	25	12
Nagato	1920(1936)	38,000	8 16-in	16 5·5-in	8 5-in	25	11½
Mutsu	1921(1936)	38,000	8 16-in	16 5·5-in	8 5-in	25	11½
Fast battleships							
Yamato	1941	65,000	9 18·1-in	12 6·1-in	12 5-in	27	16
Musashi	1942	65,000	9 18·1-in	12 6·1-in	12 5-in	27	16

N.B. The *Hyuga* and *Ise* were converted to 'battleship aircraft carriers' in 1943.

USSR

Old battleships

Oktyabrskaya Revolyutsia	1914	23,000	12 12-in	12 4·7-in		23	9
Parizhskaya Kommuna	1914	23,000	12 12-in	16 4·7-in		23	9
Marat	1914	23,000	12 12-in	16 4·7-in		23	9

N.B. At various times in their careers these ships were named respectively *Gangut, Sevastopol,* and *Petropavlovsk*.

USA

Old battleships

Arkansas	1912(1926)	26,000	12 12-in	16 5-in	8 3-in	21	11
New York	1914(1927)	27,000	10 14-in	16 5-in	8 3-in	21	12
Texas	1914(1927)	27,000	10 14-in	16 5-in	8 3-in	21	12
Nevada	1916(1929/43)	29,000	10 14-in	12 5-in	8 5-in	20	13½
Oklahoma	1916(1929)	29,000	10 14-in	12 5-in	8 5-in	20	13½
Pennsylvania	1916(1931/43)	33,000	12 14-in	12 5-in	8 5-in	21	14
Arizona	1916(1931)	33,000	12 14-in	12 5-in	8 5-in	21	14

Name	Completion year (rebuilding completion in brackets)	Tonnage	GUNS				Speed in knots	Armour (maximum thickness of side belt in inches)
			Main	Secondary	Heavy AA			

Name	Completion year (rebuilding completion in brackets)	Tonnage	Main	Secondary	Heavy AA	Speed in knots	Armour (maximum thickness of side belt in inches)
USA, Old battleships—*continued*							
Mississippi	1917(1932)	33,000	12 14-in	12 5-in	8 5-in	21	14
New Mexico	1918(1933)	33,000	12 14-in	12 5-in	8 5-in	21	14
Idaho	1919(1934)	33,000	12 14-in	12 5-in	8 5-in	21	14
Tennessee	1920(1943)	32,000	12 14-in	12 5-in	8 5-in	21	14
California	1921(1944)	32,000	12 14-in	12 5-in	8 5-in	21	14
Maryland	1921	32,000	8 16-in	12 5-in	8 5-in	21	16
Colorado	1923	32,000	8 16-in	12 5-in	8 5-in	21	16
West Virginia	1923(1944)	32,000	8 16-in	12 5-in	8 5-in	21	16

N.B. In ships rebuilt during the war, 5-inch dual-purpose guns replaced the previous secondary and A.A. guns.

			Fast battleships				
North Carolina	1941	37,000	9 16-in	20 5-in DP		28	12
Washington	1941	37,000	9 16-in	20 5-in DP		28	12
South Dakota	1942	37,000	9 16-in	20 5-in DP		28	12¼
Indiana	1942	37,000	9 16-in	20 5-in DP		28	12¼
Massachusetts	1942	37,000	9 16-in	20 5-in DP		28	12¼
Alabama	1942	37,000	9 16-in	20 5-in DP		28	12¼

USA, Fast battleships—continued

Iowa	1943	46,000	9 16-in	20 5-in DP	33	12¼
New Jersey	1943	46,000	9 16-in	20 5-in DP	33	12¼
Missouri	1944	46,000	9 16-in	20 5-in DP	33	12¼
Wisconsin	1944	46,000	9 16-in	20 5-in DP	33	12¼
Alaska	1944	28,000	9 12-in	12 5-in DP	33	10½
Guam	1944	28,000	9 12-in	12 5-in DP	33	10½

N.B. Perhaps on the principle that it is better to be hung for a sheep or white elephant, the *Alaska* and *Guam* were always described as 'large cruisers'.

Notes to this table

D.P. signifies a dual-purpose gun. However, most deck-mounted medium weapons had a limited anti-aircraft capacity. Tonnages are 'standard displacement'; some are only approximate, because most navies understated them and only crude corrections can be applied. Speeds are nominal and differ usually from the speeds obtainable under the various conditions of service. Maximum thickness of side armour is only indicative; deck armour and the distribution and extent of armour were equally important.

Select Bibliography

BBC Television Documentary Programme 'Target Tirpitz' (written and presented by Ludovic Kennedy, produced by Edward Mirzoeff).

Beesly, Patrick, *Very Special Intelligence,* Hamish Hamilton, London 1977.

Benson, James and Warren, C. E. T., *Above Us the Waves,* Harrap, London 1964.

Brown, David, *Tirpitz: The Floating Fortress,* Arms and Armour Press, London 1977.

Frere-Cook, Gervis, *The Attacks on the Tirpitz,* Ian Allan, London 1973.

Howarth, David, *The Shetland Bus,* Nelson, London 1953.

Irving, David, *The Destruction of PQ 17,* Cassells, London, 1968.

Mordal, Jacques and Vulliez, Albert, *Battleship Scharnhorst,* Hutchinson, London 1958.

Peillard, Léonce, *Sink the Tirpitz,* Jonathan Cape, London.

Public Record office, ADM 199/347; 644. ADM 223/36; 50; 87. DEFE 3/79; 86; 87; 88; 110; 342.

Roskill, Captain S. W., *The War at Sea,* HMSO, London 1956–61.

Woodward, David, *The Tirpitz,* William Kimber, London 1953.

Index

FOURTEEN MINUTES

BY JAMES CROALL

On 28th May, 1914, the *Empress of Ireland*, a 14,000 ton Canadian Pacific ocean liner, sailed from Quebec to her doom. Only hours into her voyage she ran into thick fog on the St Lawrence River, and collided with the Norwegian collier *Storstad*. Within fourteen minutes the vast liner had sunk to her watery grave. Over a thousand people were drowned.

In this dramatic reconstruction of the events leading up to the disaster, James Croall describes the scenes of terror, panic and heroism based on personal accounts from the remaining survivors. The tragedy of the *Empress of Ireland* rivals that of the *Titanic* and the *Lusitania* in the sheer magnitude of victims claimed and it is only now that the baffling mystery of the collision can fully be revealed.

HISTORY   0 7221 2548 8   £1.25